D0122053

PLAY BY PLAY

PLAY *BY* PLAY

BASEBALL, RADIO AND LIFE

IN THE

LAST CHANCE LEAGUE

NEAL CONAN

Crown Publishers • New York

Published by Crown Publishers, New York, New York.
Member of the Crown Publishing Group, a division of Random House, Inc.

www.randomhouse.com

CROWN is a trademark and the Crown colophon is a registered trademark of
Random House, Inc.

Printed in the United States of America

Design by Cynthia Dunne

Library of Congress Cataloging-in-Publication Data
Conan, Neal.
Play by play: baseball, radio and life in the last chance league / by Neal Conan.
    1. Atlantic League (Baseball league). 2. Aberdeen Arsenal (Baseball team).
            3. Radio and baseball. I. Title.
    GV875.A8 C66   2002
    796.357'0975—dc21   2002001650

ISBN 0-609-60871-1

10 9 8 7 6 5 4 3 2 1

First Edition

For Liane, Casey and Connor
And Woodie, Jane and Hob

Contents

PLAY BY PLAY

Introduction

*I*n early April 2000, just after the major league teams broke their spring training camps and headed north, a brand-new baseball club assembled on one of those recently deserted fields in Florida. The Aberdeen Arsenal consisted of manager Darrell Evans, coaches Rick Wise and Dan DiPace, trainer Jay Tharpe and twenty-five players. Many of them were surprised to be there. They were among the last guys cut as the big-league teams and their affiliated minor league squads trimmed their rosters. After years in organized baseball, they had just been told that they were too old or too slow or just not good enough. For them, the Arsenal represented a chance, maybe a last chance, to prove themselves and play their way back.

Aberdeen was a new franchise in the three-year-old Atlantic League, one of the upstart independent leagues that are challenging the vertical monopoly of professional baseball. They play by the same rules and pay about the same as the affiliated minor leagues, but they're outside the farm system of Class A, Double A and Triple A teams that develops and funnels talent for the major leagues. Or, as more than a few noted as they looked around at their new teammates, this sure ain't organized baseball.

The Arsenal represented a new chance for me, too. After more than thirty years in radio news, I was about to begin again as a play by play broadcaster. Like a rookie ballplayer, if I performed well enough, I might catch the attention of a major league team and move up. Nervous and excited, I joined the team in Aberdeen, or, more accurately, in nearby Bel Air, Maryland. Our ballpark was thirty-two miles and a world away from Camden Yards in Baltimore.

My road to baseball began on the Red Line of the Washington, D.C., subway system. Every day for many years, I rode to Gallery Place and walked a couple of blocks to work at National Public Radio. I am lucky to have an interesting and challenging job, but after a quarter century, just about anything can feel a little confining. For the previous three seasons, though, I could get off one stop early, at Metro Center, and transfer to my other life. I'd just go downstairs, switch to the Orange Line, ride that all the way out to New Carrollton and grab a taxi to baseball.

In a studio at NPR, my only window looks into a darkened control room served by an entourage of technicians, directors and producers. At the ballpark, the radio booth commands a huge expanse of supernatural green. I work by myself amid thousands, all happy to escape to a place where we all know the rules of the game. In contrast to most things in life, baseball provides important certainties: almost everything important happens out in full view, success is measured to three decimal places and at the end of the day, everybody knows the score.

Starting in 1997, I took the subway and the taxi to Prince George's Stadium, the home of the Bowie Baysox, the Double A

Eastern League affiliate of the Baltimore Orioles. The intimacy and friendliness of minor league baseball was a revelation. Some major league ballplayers are arrogant idiots, but in the minors, very few are rich or spoiled enough to spurn a kid with an autograph book. There is more respect for the game and for the coaches and managers and umpires. The lack of attitude and affordable prices have fueled a boom—this is the golden age of minor league baseball.

The independent leagues that have sprung up over the past decade are notoriously risky enterprises, a throwback to the wildcat days of baseball where individual teams and entire leagues can vanish overnight. For me, this was a long, long drop from the major leagues of broadcast journalism at NPR.

But there would be one constant—radio.

Like everybody else, I listened to radio my whole life, but I took a special interest only when some unusual voices caught my attention. This was the spring of 1966, my junior year in high school. Earlier that year my family moved into Manhattan from the suburbs of New Jersey. My father, a doctor, opened an office on the ground floor of a new high-rise, and our apartment was on the fourteenth floor of the same building. Since I was away at boarding school and presumed to be headed off to college afterward, my parents saved the substantial expense of an extra room upstairs: when I was home from school, I would sleep on a fold-out bed down in the office. I then screwed up the master plan by managing to get myself kicked out of school. That spring, I found myself at a new school in a new city.

Downstairs, in my father's office, there was a KLH FM table radio. In the daytime, it wafted soothing music through the waiting room; by night, it was my entertainment system. The radio stations I knew were all on the AM dial, so I had to explore. In those days, FM had a tiny audience comprised largely of audiophiles—hi-fi freaks—who appreciated the superior quality of the signal and listened to classical music, or the easy-listening junk that wallpapered offices like my dad's. One of the first things I noticed on FM was that the announcers were different. Their voices were deeper and slower, their accents tonier, not at all like the breathless rock-'em sock-'em jocks on the AM side. Both deliveries, though, were highly stylized.

Alone in the empty office one night, I heard something else—people who sounded like people. Men (and women!) who used the rhythms and patterns of everyday speech, who made mistakes and corrected themselves, who joked with each other and laughed and groaned. They didn't address the audience in the patronizing tones of the classical FM announcers or scream like the AM rockers. And they *cared.*

I had stumbled across the first public radio on-air fundraiser. WBAI-FM, a listener-sponsored station owned by the Pacifica Foundation, had run out of money. With the wolves at the door, their only recourse was to go on the air and beg. Nobody had ever done this before, so all kinds of people who normally worked behind the scenes went on the air and talked. And talked. It was unbelievably tedious at times, but there was passion and drama, too. These people believed in what they were doing, and they wanted—no, needed—me to join. This was real. Would they make that goal, get all the phone lines ringing, would they survive?

When they did, it took me months to find the station again. Once the marathon ended, WBAI went back to regular programs and its own cadre of golden-voiced announcers reading scripted copy. I found the sound again after midnight, when hipster Bob Fass broadcast *Radio Unnameable,* then in the mornings with the disarmingly cranky Larry Josephson, and on Saturday nights with Steve Post. When the second May Day marathon came up in the spring of my senior year, I was at the station answering telephones. I more or less moved in to the station over the following summer, pestered people until they taught me some basic skills, and finally convinced Steve Post, WBAI's chief announcer, to let me take a shot at announcing.

Steve sat me down in the black high-backed chair behind the console, made sure I knew which switches to throw and which dials to turn, pulled down the microphone and left me alone. In a few minutes, the tape that was then on the air would run out. My job was to stop the tape machine, open my mike, identify the station, read a one-line introduction and start the next tape. I would be live for about fifteen seconds. My hands shook as the tape ran out. I could barely control them enough to flip the switch. I opened the mike, took a breath and wet my pants.

The valve closed at almost the same instant it opened, but the same signal went to my larynx and my words emerged in a strangled squeak. Sitting just out of sight in the next room, Steve shook his head. "This kid," he said, "is never going to make it."

Despite that inauspicious debut, I stuck with radio and announcing, and since I was willing to work for free and found no task too demeaning, WBAI let me stick around. By the time May came around again, Post let me fill the overnight hours, where I could do little damage. I was on the air.

Many years later, I wondered when I'd lost the passion. You can't wet yourself every time you go on the radio, but if there isn't a little fear, a tightening around the throat, what's the point? I felt that thrill again when I started to do play by play, and I realized that I'd heard those human voices before, too. Mel Allen, Phil Rizzuto and Red Barber had been my radio pals for many years growing up and had always spoken like real people. Sure, they had their mannerisms, but baseball announcers, with all that time to fill, told stories and swapped jokes. They used a conversational tone that gave them space to get excited; they shouted when shouting was called for. And they *cared.*

To do this, I would have to abandon the comfortable cocoon of family and friends and whatever reputation I may have earned. And there could be no half measures; if I stepped off the cliff in April, there would be no place to land until late September. Throw in the fact that I'd be making about as much as I had thirty years before, and who could resist? It was time to take a risk, step off the subway one stop early, and take the road to baseball.

Long Pond, Massachusetts
September 5, 2001

1

OPENING NIGHT

ABERDEEN ARSENAL OPENING DAY ROSTER						
PITCHERS	**B/T**	**HT.**	**WT.**	**D.O.B.**	**BIRTHPLACE/ RESIDENCE**	**1999 CLUB**
Alberro, Jose	R/R	6'2"	190	6/29/69	Arecibo, PR/ Arecibo, PR	Toledo (AAA), Jacksonville (AA), Calgary (AAA)
Bacon, Matt	R/R	6'5"	200	4/18/76	Peoria, IL/ Peoria, IL	Lancaster (A)
Bair, Andy	L/L	6'5"	250	1/12/77	Baltimore, MD/ Manchester, MD	Did Not Play
Callahan, Justin	R/R	5'10"	180	1/1/77	Turnersville, NJ/ Turnersville, NJ	Gloucester CC
Garcia, Miguel	R/R	6'2"	175	2/15/75	Santiago, DR/ Santiago, DR	Did Not Play
Hurst, Doug	R/R	5'11"	200	2/23/76	Pensacola, FL/ Pensacola, FL	Did Not Play
Miranda, Angel	L/L	6'1"	195	11/9/69	Arecibo, PR/ Arecibo, PR	Lehigh Valley (ATL)
Olszewski, Eric	R/R	6'2"	195	1/1/75	Houston, TX/ Spring, TX	Atlantic City (ATL)
Scott, Ron	L/L	5'10"	195	7/24/71	Sharon, PA/ Sarasota, FL	Did Not Play
Stark, Zac	R/L	6'6"	225	8/7/74	Kansas City, MO/ Nashville, TN	Lancaster (A)
Tucker, Julien	L/R	6'7"	200	4/19/72	Montreal, PQ/ Châteauguay, PQ	Birmingham (AA)

CATCHERS

Andreopoulos, Alex	L/R	5'10" 190	8/19/72	Toronto, ON/ Toronto, ON	Louisville (AAA)
Healy, Liam	R/R	6'0" 185	12/21/76	Baltimore, MD/ Baltimore, MD	Spokane (IND)

INFIELDERS

Poss, Johnny	R/R	5'11" 180	10/5/76	Columbia, MD/ Bowie, MD	Canton (IND)
Rosario, Victor	R/R	6'2" 190	8/26/66	Hato Mayor DelRey, DR/Tampa, FL	Taiwan
Sanchez, Yuri	S/R	6'1" 165	11/11/73	Moca, DR/ Lynn, MA	Binghamton (AA)
Steed, David	R/R	6'1" 205	2/25/73	Villa Rica, GA/ Little Rock, AR	Albuquerque (AAA)
Taylor, Matt	L/R	6'0" 180	3/7/74	Berkeley, CA/ Richmond, CA	Nashua (ATL)
Wolff, Mike	L/L	6'3" 205	2/17/74	South Bend, IN/ Granger, IN	El Paso (AA)

OUTFIELDERS

Fowler, Maleke	R/R	5'11" 180	8/11/75	Baton Rouge, LA/ Baton Rouge, LA	Amarillo (IND)
Isom, Johnny	R/R	5'11" 210	8/9/73	Urbana, IL/ Fort Worth, TX	Rochester (AAA), Bowie (AA)
Kelley, Erskine	R/R	6'4" 220	2/27/71	Freeport, NY/ Stroudsburg, PA	Allentown (IND)
Lewis, T. R.	R/R	6'0" 180	4/17/71	Jacksonville, FL/ Jacksonville, FL	Did Not Play
Martinez, Gil	R/R	6'0" 200	3/30/68	San Juan, PR/ San Juan, PR	Somerset (ATL)
Perez, Danny	R/R	5'9" 175	2/26/71	El Paso, TX/ El Paso, TX	Lehigh Valley (ATL)

MANAGER, COACHES, STAFF

Evans, Darrell	Manager
Wise, Rick	Pitching Coach
DiPace, Dan	First-Base Coach
Tharpe, Jay	Trainer
Lebrun, Donald	Clubhouse Manager

*O*pening night, and I can't get on the air. Peter Kirk, who owns half the team, comes by the press box to welcome me to the organization. "I told you we'd get you a job," he says expansively, and gets a weak smile and a mumble in reply. The general manager, Keith Lupton, has bought thousands of dollars of broadcast equipment on my recommendation, and it's not working. "We'll improvise something," I tell him. "That's what we do in minor league baseball," he says, but Plan A is failing fast and we're a little short on Plan B.

Peter and Keith are on the field applauding as the public address announcer introduces the mayor, a bank president and half a dozen other dignitaries. Vi Ripken, the matriarch of Aberdeen's first family of baseball, throws the first pitch to her son Bill, the club's director of baseball operations, and the radio voice of the Aberdeen Arsenal is broadcasting a public service announcement for the Coast Guard over and over again. It's April 28, about 45 degrees, a flag-snapping wind whips through the open window in front of me and the flush of fear fogs my glasses.

Gary Helton, the manager of the radio station, works with me all afternoon to get the stubborn piece of digital technology on my end to stay connected with an inert box of wires back at WHFC-FM. These magic devices are supposed to transform a regular telephone line into a high-quality broadcast circuit, but they work only when my encoder engages his decoder. We attempt this hookup a dozen times or more and the marriage never lasts more than twenty seconds. The chief engineer is summoned to mutter incantations and wave his voltmeter solemnly over the unresponsive red metal container. We check and recheck to see that all the wires are plugged into their appropriate receptacles and make sure the power is on. A retired umpire begins to belt out an operatic rendition of the national anthem, the first game in the team's history is about to begin and my box blinks CALL DISCONNECTED. Over the phone Gary tells me, "We're cooked."

Radio's time-honored quick and dirty solution is to unscrew the mouthpiece of the telephone, take out the little microphone capsule and attach a pair of alligator clips to the metal prongs underneath. High-tech it ain't, but you can get a feed through. Except the telephone handset in the press box is one of those designer plastic jobs that can only be opened with a crowbar, and as I start to look around for one, Gary tells me that the radio station doesn't have a phone coupler anyway. In thirty years in radio, I have never *heard* of a station that couldn't put a telephone call on the air.

"Play ball!" Eleven hundred throats cheer. In the press box, one croaks, "Is there nothing we can do?"

The engineer then earns his fee. He tells me to call the extension in the station's on-air studio on the press box phone. He gets my call up on the tiny, tinny speakerphone, puts a microphone on that, and we're on. Sort of. This may well be the worst audio quality ever broadcast on FM radio, and I proceed to embellish it with some truly miserable play by play. In my panic to get the jury-rig on the air, I see a guy strike out, but somehow fail to notice that a player in road gray is already standing on second base. The player I've just announced as the second batter in the visitors' lineup then hits a single and the phantom runner pops into my consciousness as he rounds third and heads to the plate. Oh, my.

Running away with a minor league baseball team seemed like such a good idea a month ago.

I was no longer just fifty, I was going on fifty-one. My daughter and her boyfriend drove a Ryder truck up from college to move her stuff to Florida. I have a wonderful job as a radio news correspondent and host that's allowed me to go all kinds of places and do interesting things, but I was bored. Probably with myself. Call it burnout or midlife crisis, but after Whitewater, Newt, Monica and impeachment, I was weary. With bleak months of what promised to be a joyless presidential election campaign stretching ahead, I thought it miraculous when Keith Lupton called with a chance to broadcast baseball instead. This was fate. I cashed in twenty-three years of tenure at National Public Radio and abandoned wife, children, yard, cat and a career inside the Washington Beltway to punch my ticket to the small time. This summer, my audience would be measured in dozens, not millions. Accustomed to broadcasting with the help of two technicians, a producer and a director in a state-of-the-art studio, I would be a one-man traveling band. I called up the team's schedule on my computer. In late July I could anchor three nights of the Republican

National Convention live from the First Union Center in Philadelphia or call play by play of a three-game set against the Bluefish at Harbor Yard in Bridgeport, Connecticut.

Baseball sounded like a lot more fun.

And there was a symmetry that reinforced the sense of kismet. Four years earlier, I was in a hotel room in Chicago cramming for the first night of the Democratic National Convention with the ball game on the radio. As the broadcast got under way, I realized how closely what I did as the anchor resembled play by play. Each night in Chicago, I would open the live coverage with a short setup, go over the lineup of speakers and events, exchange banter with an analyst and, once things got under way, describe the action as it unfolded before me. Substitute Wrigley Field for the United Center and the subject changes, but not the technique. The skills were transferable.

Until that moment, my dream had been to play baseball, not to broadcast it. Like every kid, I'd announce aloud as I caught the tennis balls I bounced off the wall in the school-yard, but the radio voice I heard in my head wasn't mine—it was Mel Allen's, describing my over-the-shoulder catch that saved the seventh game of the World Series. How ABOUT that? I was never much of a player, though. In Little League and later, at school, I played second base. At that level, second base can be read to mean that I had no arm at all. I was a pesky little hitter as long as I saw fastballs, but even the mildest of breaking pitches triggered a powerful impulse to pull my left foot out of the line of fire and step directly into what's still known as "the bucket." I can honestly say I've never experienced a knee-buckling curveball, because I never stayed in there long enough to get jelly legs. My biggest strength was an unending stream of infield chatter, which, come to think of it, was better training for radio than baseball. Much later, embarrassment limited my participation on the company softball team to a couple of cameos. But after three decades of live radio—elections, wars, congressional hearings, parades, speeches, trials and a couple of inaugurations—I listened to that ball game and thought, "I can do this."

The idea percolated for a few months. That winter Peter Angelos, the new owner of the Baltimore Orioles, got into an extended controversy with the team's brilliant play by play man, Jon Miller, and the name of Miller's agent came up frequently in the papers. If Ron Shapiro was good enough for Jon Miller, I figured, he was good enough for me. I wrote him a letter explaining who I was and that I wanted to take a shot at baseball. Be more specific, he replied. Okay. Might as well shoot the moon. My goal, I wrote boldly, was to broadcast in the major leagues in three or four years. As a first step, I wanted the chance to do a few games in the minor leagues somewhere, put a tape together and get his opinion on my prospects.

It turned out that Ron Shapiro listens to NPR and knew who I was. He's also a man who loves to help people. He put me in touch with a friend of his, Jon Danos, general manager of the Bowie Baysox, an Orioles affiliate in the Double A Eastern League that plays about thirty miles from my house in the Maryland suburbs of Washington, D.C.

Despite the proximity, I'd never heard of the Baysox, much less attended a game. Growing up in and around New York City, the minors were never part of my baseball culture. Intellectually, I knew there was a continental network of leagues and teams out there somewhere, but, apart from the occasional glance at the Down on the Farm feature in my Yankees program, I didn't give it a lot of thought. I regarded the "bushes" as nothing more than a stepping-stone, an early chapter in a hero's biography.

On a cold, clear day in late March 1997, a taxi turned hesitantly off Route 301 in Bowie, onto a road that seemed to lead nowhere. The directions promised that this dubious stretch of blacktop would take us to Prince George's Stadium, but a long slow drive with nothing but bare trees to either side made me wonder if we'd taken a wrong turn. The driver was no help—he'd never heard of the ballpark or the team.

Eventually, we wound past some parking lots and up to the gate of a modern brick-faced structure. I went through the Office door to the left and, since I was early for my appointment, asked if it would be okay to take a look around. I'm not sure what I expected—the exterior sure didn't look anything like *Bull Durham*. As I stepped out of the Authorized Personnel Only door, the first glimpse of glorious green drew me across the concourse, past the press box and down the concrete steps to the field boxes behind home plate. Nestled in trees I could now see were in bud, a handsomely proportioned and meticulously groomed ballfield spread out in front of me. The eight-foot-tall outfield fence was draped with advertising. Another fence three times as high rose about ten feet beyond and it, too, hawked the services of local banks, plumbers and car dealers. The big scoreboard in left center field was blank, the speakers strung on wires over the stands hung silent, but the place pulsed with energy and life. My summers would never be the same.

A few minutes later, Jon Danos introduced me to Dave Collins, the team's public relations director and play by play broadcaster. Dave is a tall, thin man, about thirty-five years old at the time, with a deep baritone and unruly blond hair. Jon was an NPR listener; Dave wasn't, but he understood that I had a lot of radio experience and said he thought games always sounded better with two voices. Jon is younger than Dave, bald and fit; a cancer survivor, I'd learn later.

All the Baysox games are carried on a small station in Annapolis, but Jon explained that this season, weekend games would also be on a big AM station in Washington, a market he hoped to develop, and he thought that my participation might help make an impression in D.C. They agreed to let me come to some early-season games to learn the ropes, "broadcast" a game or two into a tape recorder, and if that was okay, we'd see about going on the air. It wasn't exactly the keys to the radio booth in Yankee Stadium, but it was a start.

I'd actually tried to start earlier. I remembered a story Joe Garagiola used to tell, about his transition from the playing field to the broadcast booth. He said he spent a lot of time in his den, calling games as he watched on TV. So, with the Yanks and Orioles scheduled to play in spring training, I clipped the team rosters from the newspaper and set myself up with a cassette tape recorder in front of the TV in my basement. Before the first half inning was over, I had new respect for Garagiola. It is impossible to call a game on TV. As soon as I started to describe something, the camera would cut away. I couldn't locate the statistics I needed. I'd glance down to remind myself how many RBIs Rafael Palmeiro knocked home last season, only to hear the crack of a bat and know that I was missing the next play. Quick shot of the bullpen, somebody's warming up and there's no way to figure out who, or why. Fly ball to left, who's that playing out there again? A shot of the rookie short-stop, another quick look down for his first name, just long enough to lose track of the ball-and-strike count.

Worst of all was my scorekeeping. Along with acne, I'd developed an elaborate scoring system as a youth. Mine was a complicated and individualized accounting method that left me prepared to reconstruct every play in detail. This was about as useless an activity as can be imagined, but now those long hours were vindicated. I was sure this was one part of the business that would be no problem. Game conditions exposed a few flaws. The penmanship I used to enter the lineups was a tribute to clean living and the Palmer method, but under pressure small, neat notations grew hideously large and messy. Fours became indistinguishable from nines. More than ever, I needed to know whether that flyout to left back in the third inning had been a threatening drive toward the alley or a harmless pop-up, but there wasn't room enough or time to mark down the appropriate squiggles.

Garagiola said he'd play his tapes over and over to learn his strengths and weaknesses. In hopes of preserving a little bit of confidence, I never listened to mine at all.

Soon after the season started, I headed out to Prince George's Stadium for my first Baysox game. Dave Collins showed me the thick package of statistics provided daily by Howe Sportsdata, the record keepers of minor league baseball, and the even heftier sheaf of game notes that he'd worked up on his own. Just about any number you'd need is buried in there somewhere, though finding it at the right moment remained a challenge. Dave also showed me a simple and hugely helpful device for my score book, a little diamond I could draw in above each lineup to show the opposing team's defense. "Ground ball to short," glance down, "Ojeda's got it, over to first," glance down, "Kirgan makes the stretch." And at the ballpark, there was that big scoreboard out in left center to keep track of a few other important items for me. Glance up, "Two out."

When I settled myself into the stands with my tape recorder

the next time out, I encountered another major problem: I knew nothing about any of these players. Calling the TV game in my basement, I had well-publicized stars like Derek Jeter to talk about. I knew going in that Jeter liked to turn on the first pitch and often used an inside-out swing when he was down in the count. I knew he'd grown up in Michigan and New Jersey, I knew that he'd played his Double A ball here in the Eastern League, I could rattle off last year's batting average from memory. Augie Ojeda? Beyond the cold numbers, I was utterly ignorant, and the fact that he was hitting .150 coming into the game can be used only so many times. And was that o-HAY-duh or o-HEE-duh?

This time, I worked up the nerve to listen to the tape. There were a lot of awkward silences and an unconscionable number of "uhs," but there were also some moments. After one or two more games in the stands, Jon came by to ask how it was coming.

"Okay."

The thing was, he said, Dave's son A. J. was about to graduate from kindergarten and the ceremony didn't start till six or so and it looked like he might miss the first couple of innings next Thursday; did I think I might be ready to fill in?

I can honestly thank the American education system for giving me my big break in baseball.

That very night Dave started to break me in. I was off the tape recorder and on the air. He turned over the mike in the top of the fourth, but sat in with me to help out and correct my mistakes as gently as possible. When he resumed as the lead voice an inning later, I stayed on to provide color. I did two innings the next game—one alone—and three the night before my solo.

On the big day, I got to the ballpark two hours early to learn that my old friend Noah Adams had ratted me out to *The Washington Post*. Marc Fisher, the paper's radio writer, came out with a photographer to do a feature for the Style section. He asked whether he was making me nervous, and I told him I couldn't imagine being more nervous than I was already, so we might as well go ahead with it.

Baysox third baseman Mike Berry made the pregame show for hitting three home runs the weekend before against the Portland Sea Dogs, the same club that was providing the opposition tonight. After revisiting his big night up in Maine, I asked about his older brother, Sean, who played third base in the big leagues for the Houston Astros—I was learning. I wrote out a short introduction to open the broadcast, looked up when I finished reading it, took a deep breath and stepped off the cliff.

Fisher, who was being very kind, observed in his story the next day that my delivery was "a little high and tight" but I managed to hang on to it and the game was a novice announcer's dream. The Sea Dogs got a run on a couple of hits in the second, but otherwise, it was a fast-moving pitchers' duel with no long rallies, bizarre plays or arcane scoring decisions. Five innings raced by before Dave arrived, and he took over just in time as Portland proceeded to bat around.

The debut was certainly no better than okay, but the good luck to attract a reporter meant I could pay the Baysox back for their kindness by bringing them a little publicity in Washington. Fisher's story led the *Post* Style section with a big picture above the fold. The headline was essentially "Man Bites Dog." "Playing in a New Field"; the caption read, "An NPR Newsman Takes a Swing at Baseball Announcing."

I ended up doing more than thirty games with Dave Collins that summer. The following season, I stacked up a bunch of vacation time and traveled with the team for a couple of months. Ducking out of work early as many weeknights as I could and giving over my weekends, I got in forty games the year after that. Even so, after a three-year unpaid apprenticeship, I had yet to broadcast the equivalent of one full season. I thought I was pretty good but knew that if I wanted to find out how good, I needed to do this every day, by myself, for a whole season.

Peter Kirk's Maryland Baseball owned the Baysox and two other Orioles affiliates, the Frederick Keys and the Delmarva Shorebirds. Their offices were at the ballpark in Bowie, so Keith Lupton, the group's start-up specialist, was familiar with my work when the organization went into a partnership with the Ripken family to bring professional baseball to Aberdeen, Maryland. They got an expansion team in the upstart Atlantic League, an independent circuit unaffiliated with any of the major league teams. Originally, the new club wasn't expected to begin play until the following season, by which time a brand-new stadium would be ready to house it. The decision to start in 2000 meant that all kinds of arrangements, even the team's home field, would have to be improvised at the last minute and a broadcast deal was not at the top of Keith's must-do list.

There are only two commercial stations near Aberdeen, an FM country rocker that didn't want to break format for baseball and an AM oldies station that was a well-established beacon in the Baltimore Orioles Radio Network. "Captain" Jim McMahan, who owns the AMer, is close to the Ripken family, president of the Ripken Museum and would serve as the new team's public address announcer. He had reportedly offered to dump the O's—the signal from the big team's flagship station in Baltimore was audible almost everywhere in town, anyway—to carry the local team's games, but Maryland Baseball decided it would be unwise to risk the wrath of the notoriously mercurial Peter Angelos. No deal.

Then at the last minute, a public radio station made a proposal. WHFC is a small nonprofit FM station licensed to Harford Community College. The school had already leased its ballfield, Thomas Run Park, as a temporary home field for the professional team. Gary Helton said he'd been hired to get the station onto the map; he saw Arsenal baseball as an opportunity to generate some publicity, pick up new listeners and, with any luck, develop a stream of revenue from what we in public radio call underwriting and everybody else calls ads.

The first big hurdle for me was money. My wife, Liane, and I had a son going into his senior year of high school as well as a daughter in college, and this job would mean a precipitous drop in salary. I would earn $75 a game, better than Bowie, but not exactly network scale. I knew I was more than halfway home when I got Liane to laugh. "It wasn't easy," I told her, "but I've managed to find a sector of the broadcast industry that pays less than public radio." She told me to go for it.

I went on to hurdle number two: Aberdeen is too far away. There's no way to commute from my house in Bethesda. I'd be away even on home dates. A hundred forty games. Five months. She swallowed hard—bless her—and said that if this was something I needed to do, go do it. Bruce Drake, my boss at NPR, was less than pleased to have to reshuffle plans for the summer's political coverage to accommodate a sudden request for a leave of absence, but he laughed, too. Which is how I found myself sweating play by play into a telephone handset on a cold night at Thomas Run Park.

Rain washed out a practice the day before, so opening night was my first look at the squad. Trailing 1–0 after their first half inning, the Arsenal got their first hit, their first run and their first lead in rapid succession. The honor of the first hit went to outfielder Gil Martinez, who stroked a clean single to center in the bottom of the first.

All I had in the way of scouting notes on Martinez and his teammates came from Adam Gladstone, officially director of team operations and effectively the director of player personnel. Adam was an Atlantic League umpire in 1998, the first year of the league's existence, and he looked the part. He's a stout young man with straight black hair and a cheerful demeanor on a big, square head. The following season, he graduated to a front-office job with the Lehigh Valley Black Diamonds, and after he moved over to Aberdeen he found ways to bring several ex–Black Diamonds along with him. Accustomed to thankless tasks from his days in blue, Adam was the guy in charge of everything nobody else was in charge of, plus a bunch of other stuff. Amid a flurry of phone calls, he found twenty minutes to give me thumbnails.

Gil Martinez, I was able to tell my listeners, was a thirty-two-year-old from San Juan who played briefly in the Red Sox organization and later participated in the Pan American Games as a member of Puerto Rico's national fast-pitch softball team. He batted over .300 last year as a part-timer for the Somerset Patriots, who left him exposed in the Atlantic League's expansion draft where the Arsenal claimed him in the fourth round. It was a steal. Martinez's line drive was an omen; he'd spend the summer slashing singles and his name was always listed among the league's leading hitters.

Starting pitcher Angel Miranda was, Adam advised, the ace of the staff. The stylish left-hander was from Arecibo, Puerto Rico, which gave me an opening to talk about the enormous radio telescope for which his hometown is world-famous. I couldn't remember which James Bond movie climaxed inside the big dish, but one of them did. Even better, Miranda had four years' experience in the big leagues with the Milwaukee Brewers, plenty to yak about there, and he was pitching against his former team: he threw for the Black Diamonds last season and was one of the top pitchers in the Atlantic League.

On this ever-chillier evening, Miranda was having difficulty with his touch on the breaking ball. He hung a couple of fat pitches over the heart of the plate that were ripped for home runs, but he did it with nobody on base and turned a one-run lead over to the bullpen. Tall, thin Julien Tucker was the first reliever to come in. My notes from Adam on him amounted to a single word: gas. The kid threw very, very hard and got the job done. The home team tacked on another run in the late innings and the Arsenal took a two-run edge into the ninth.

A thriller for the first game! From the bullpen down the left-field line, Jose Alberro came in to close it out. Alberro was another Puerto Rican, also from Arecibo, and another former major leaguer—he'd played with Bill Ripken on the Texas Rangers. And like Miranda and a lot of players coming north after winter ball in the Caribbean and spring training in Florida, he was unprepared for the cold of a mid-Atlantic April. His best pitch, a hard sinker, didn't dive much that night. A flurry of hits and walks developed into a rally and then into a meltdown. Arsenal fielders fumbled ground balls and compounded their mistakes with late, wild throws. Before the panic subsided, six Black Diamonds crossed the plate on four hits and three errors. The game was gone.

It was a devastating loss; but the first thing you learn about baseball is that it's a long season. On the postgame show that night, I reminded listeners that there were 139 more to play.

Surely there would be better days for Miranda, Alberro and the Arsenal.

The next night, we got all the broadcast equipment to work. Aberdeen blasted Lehigh Valley for ten hits and ten runs in the first six innings and took a three-run lead into the ninth. They blew that one, too.

The defense was primarily responsible for the second collapse. Two crucial errors led to four unearned runs. That made it eight errors in the first two games and a few other misplays that the official scorer overlooked. Searching for something positive, I talked a lot about the promise of the new club's terrific-looking offense. Later I learned that manager Darrell Evans and coach Dan DiPace went through their roster that night over a drink or two in the bar of the Sheraton Four Points Hotel. Two brutal games removed from the sunny optimism of spring training, they shook their heads over their squad of castoffs: the slow and the wild, the unlucky, the injured, the overlooked and the knuckleheads. "There's a reason they're all here," they told each other.

It was an expression they would repeat at low moments over the remainder of the schedule, and it was true enough. If the pitchers could throw their best stuff with consistency, if the glove men were reliable and could hit even a little, if the hitters had more power, if surgery hadn't robbed this pitcher of five miles an hour on his fastball, or that outfielder of his speed, if somebody had taught them properly years ago, they'd be in big-league organizations. For one reason or another, they all washed out. To me, that made them more interesting than most of the players I'd seen in Double A in Bowie. Those guys were all on a clear road to Cooperstown and while they'd had their share of sore arms and torn ligaments, they only *thought* they knew adversity. Their goal was simple: Onward!

Things are more complicated in the independent leagues. There were a lot of guys determined to make it back to an organization, some just hanging on, some doing the only thing they knew how to do. They were older, for the most part, literally and figuratively scarred by injury and failure. Everyone had a story.

It turned out that there were reasons that Darrell and Dan were there. And over time, I realized there were reasons why the radio guy was there, too.

The next day, the first Sunday-afternoon game of the season, the Arsenal scored five times in the first inning and this time they managed to hold on to the lead. I knew they couldn't lose them all, but that first W was a relief. Left-handed starting pitcher Zac Stark went into the record books with the first win in club history, and switch-hitting second baseman Yuri Sanchez hit the club's first home run.

It's dangerous to make a lot of judgments on the basis of the first three games, but the team collected a total of 39 hits, including 12 doubles and the one homer. It was clear the Arsenal could really hit the ball.

It was equally obvious that they couldn't catch it. They committed four more errors on Sunday. Of the twelve official miscues, six originated at third base, and three different guys were responsible; this raised doubts that any of them could play the position. Just as alarming, veteran shortstop Victor Rosario showed no range at all. Sadly out of shape, he had a hard time bending over as a series of routine groundouts scooted under his halfhearted glove and on into the outfield. At second, Sanchez was in the process of a conversion from shortstop—I'd seen him play there in the Eastern League with the Binghamton Mets. He moved well, but looked indecisive on a couple of grounders and panicked on a pop fly. At first base, Mike Wolff looked sharp and saved his teammates a few more errors by scooping up most of the balls they threw in the dirt. The outfield seemed decent, though Gil Martinez in left had problems with balls hit over his head: he played exceptionally deep to compensate and allowed a couple of soft fly balls to drop in front of him for hits.

Gil's misadventures were exacerbated by the contour of the field, which sloped away on the left side. From home plate, you could see the left fielder only from the waist up. The infield had been resodded and leveled before the season and wasn't too bad, except for the edges between the dirt and the grass. Every once in a while, a ground ball would hit the lip of the outfield grass and take a crazy hop right over an infielder's head. Pitchers complained that the mound was too soft and too low and that they left the ball up in the strike zone as a result.

The most obvious Thomas Run factor, though, was the park's size. Signs on the twelve-foot chain-link fence that circled the outfield announced the dimensions as 315 feet down the foul lines and 375 to dead center, but the consensus held that the field was ten to fifteen feet shorter than that all the way around. Tom King, a writer for the *Nashua Telegraph*, would dub it "the Bel Air bandbox." If the wind was right, just about anything up in the air had a good chance to go out.

The lights were reasonably bright but mounted on poles that were too short. At night, fly balls disappeared into the darkness above the lights, and fielders could only hope to pick them up again on the way down.

But this was a wonderful place to watch a ball game. Intimacy is one of the great attractions of minor league baseball and at Thomas Run, fans were close enough to hear the zip on a fastball and eavesdrop on the infield chatter.

The press box was in a trailer set up right behind the back-stop on the third-base side. This was more than a little awkward. I had no way to judge pitches inside or outside. I could see directly up the first-base line, but the trailer wall blocked the view to my left. Anything that happened in the foul ground beyond third base, or in the left-field corner, was a mystery. On the other hand, I was close enough that my microphone could pick up the crack of the bat and the umpire's strike calls. Of course, a part of that was because there wasn't a lot of crowd noise.

Once the portable seating was installed, the team proclaimed that the field could accommodate "3,000 plus." I doubted they could fit anything close to that but, in the event, the official capacity was never tested. Opening-night attendance was 1,158. About half that number came Saturday, and Sunday afternoon it was less than 500. That was well below critical mass. People might have come with every intention to cheer their new heroes, but there just weren't enough of them to develop any enthusiasm. It was simply little knots of fans that never coalesced into a crowd. It was a little like playing baseball in secret.

WHFC's broadcast tower was visible on a low hill about half a mile beyond the right-field fence, next to a small building that housed the transmitter. Its power was listed at 1050 watts, enough, in theory, to cover sprawling, mostly agricultural Harford County and spill over into Baltimore County to the south. In theory. In practice, signal coverage was mysteriously spotty—good in some unexpectedly distant locations, impossible in some places quite nearby. It was a little like broadcasting in secret, too.

2

ATLANTIC LEAGUE STANDINGS

THROUGH GAMES OF APRIL 30, 2000

NORTH DIVISION	W	L	PCT.	GB	STREAK	LAST 10
Newark	2	1	.667	—	W 1	2–1
Nashua	2	1	.667	—	L 1	2–1
Bridgeport	2	1	.667	—	W 1	2–1
Long Island	1	2	.333	1	W 1	1–2
SOUTH DIVISION						
Lehigh Valley	2	1	.667	—	L 1	2–1
Somerset	1	2	.333	1	L 1	1–2
Atlantic City	1	2	.333	1	L 1	1–2
Aberdeen	1	2	.333	1	W 1	1–2

I don't drive. To make a long story short, I see my death behind the wheel, so I don't sit there. When I lived in New York, London and Washington, this was only mildly inconvenient; and even in the suburbs, where I live now, it's not too bad. My wife has to do all the driving chores and I have to do a lot of walking, but as long as she's willing to put up with me, it's doable.

Aberdeen does not boast much of a mass transit system and our ballfield, Thomas Run Park, was on the campus of Harford Community College, about ten miles from the office downtown. I thought some student housing might be available for the summer, but—I should have known—it's a commuter school. The address is in Bel Air, the seat of Harford County, but when I took a cab out to take a look before the season started, I found the school right on the edge of town, much closer to sleepy Churchville than to bustling downtown Bel Air.

For the first of many times, Charlie Vascellaro came to my rescue. I knew Charlie from Bowie, where he handled publicity for all three Maryland Baseball teams and now had the same duties with Aberdeen. Like many minor league teams, the Arsenal asked fans if they might be willing to house ballplayers. Some people offered a room over the garage, others a trailer, and there were a few empty nesters with kids' rooms to spare. Charlie put me in touch with Ed and Georgette Paulson, who had two extra bedrooms.

The good news was that Ed, Georgette and the house were all terrific. A couple of days after I settled in, left-handed relief pitcher Ron Scott took their other room, and he was very friendly. The bad news was that it was still seven miles away from Thomas Run. Uphill. My plan to commute to work by bicycle suddenly looked a little dubious.

The problems began right at the end of the Paulsons' driveway. They lived at the bottom of a dale and on opening day, climbing out of it was more than I could handle. I had to get off and push the bike up to the main road. Then there was a fast, scary drop down to a stream called Carsins Run, with a long, lung-spearing climb out of its valley. I hadn't been riding a lot, but assumed that my legs would be in shape from regular running. Cycling, I learned, uses an entirely different set of muscles. As I wheezed through the front gate before the first game, general manager Keith Lupton came over to ask if I was all right.

"Fine," I gasped. "No problem."

I locked my Raleigh behind the prefab garden shed that was used as an umpires' room, wobbled over to the bleachers behind home plate, sat down and put my head between my knees. I'd timed the ride to get a better idea of the commute: 56 minutes and 15 seconds. The return trip would be easier, but this was a nice cool day in April. Summer was coming, days and nights of ferocious heat and humidity, and I wondered how in the world I was going to make it up that hill forty-seven more times.

Though maybe I wouldn't need to. For the first time in many years, I seriously wondered if I might get fired.

Opening night was a tip-off. After the game, several people told me they thought I'd done pretty well "under the circumstances." The lukewarm compliments vanished with the qualifier when the equipment problems were solved. Not to put too fine a point on it, I stunk. The play by play was filled with long, awkward gaps. I was hesitant, slow and wrong so often that I seemed to be apologizing with every other breath: "Check that . . ."; "Excuse me . . ."; "I'm sorry, but . . ."

On Sunday, which was the first day game of the season, Bill Ripken agreed to join me on the air for a couple of innings, and, working with a color man again, I felt the beginnings of a little rhythm developing, the old patter coming back.

"Swing and a miss, the count goes to one ball, two strikes."

Bill said something about the pitcher setting up the guy at

the plate for a breaking ball away, and, sure enough, the next one wafted outside.

"Kelley swings and misses." I could have left well enough alone right there. "What a weak . . ." I groped for the word: "hack"? "lunge"? I couldn't say "swing" again. I swear my mouth moved of its own volition: ". . . waffle."

"A *waffle*?" Ripken was incredulous. "A weak *waffle*? Hey, why don'cha just say, 'If you're waving at me, just say hi!'" He shook his head in disbelief. "Waffle!"

This gaffe was Topic A in the press box until, a few innings later, I described a curveball as "a beautiful breaking bitch."

I looked at Keith right after I said it, and thankfully, he had the presence of mind not to laugh out loud. All you can do with one of those is to pretend you never said it and plunge on. It's so ludicrous that listeners half believe they couldn't have heard what they thought they heard anyway. The press box knew better, though, and I had a new nickname: "BB."

After the game, Keith told me that we needed to talk, and to call him at the office the next morning, before we left on the first road trip. After a long night of fretting, I phoned and we quickly agreed that I had plenty of room to improve. "I know I need to smooth it out. I'm sure I'll get better."

"Oh, sure," Keith said, "like the players."

That was unsettling. As general manager, Keith cut and traded players every day. He had people coming in for a meeting and couldn't talk. We'd go into details another time. The bus arrived like a reprieve from the governor.

On most teams, the bus leaves from the ballpark, which makes it easy to collect everybody's equipment from the clubhouse and where nobody minds if the players and coaches leave their cars in an otherwise empty lot. The Arsenal didn't have a real ballpark, the college needed all the parking spaces and there was no clubhouse. Until the school year was over and the locker room in the field house opened up, the Arsenal changed in and out of their uniforms in a tent and visiting players had to dress and shower at their hotel. Arsenal manager Darrell Evans and his coaches, Rick Wise and Dan DiPace, stayed at the same hotel, the Sheraton Four Points, and that was our point of departure.

The bus was a very nice Belgian make, a Van Hool, with plush seats and three screens for the built-in VCR, a toilet in the back and plenty of room for equipment and luggage underneath. Our driver, Bill Pike, described it as the Cadillac of buses, but there is no way to change its essential nature. A bus is uncomfortable for medium-size people like me. We had a couple of pitchers over six-five who had to coil themselves into their seats, and even then, their legs spilled over into the aisle. As we stepped up into the bus, Adam handed each of us an envelope stuffed with cash. Meal money. Players received $15 a day, staff members—and I was delighted to find that that included the radio guy—got $25. In theory this was to cover expenses, but it was also the first money I'd ever received in baseball. I was a professional now.

Adam Gladstone wanted seating to be arranged according to a strict hierarchy. The grown-ups were in front. The right front seat was reserved for the manager, and it was sacrosanct. From time to time, someone might come up to ask him a question, but no one ever sat down next to him. The coaches came next, then the trainer, Jay Tharpe, and then the radio guy. Guys with major league experience took the next best seats, players who'd reached Triple A were behind them, and the arrangement was supposed to move back into Double A and Single A sections, with a few guys who never made it out of rookie ball all the way back by the toilet.

This system unraveled immediately. Guys rearranged themselves on the basis of friendships and race and language. The bus is more than a form of transportation. It's a rolling dormitory, living room, cellular telephone booth, office, game room and movie theater. It's also a metaphor for the minor leagues. Players going down from the major leagues will complain about riding the buses again; conversely, players on the way up are delighted to get off the bus.

T. R. Lewis and David Steed brought a big cooler aboard that they'd stuffed with fresh fruit and vegetables to carry them through the nutrient-free zone of fast-food joints that fed the rest of us. The cooler top also provided space for the eternal card game. Ninety-nine percent of the time they played spades, which is a little more complicated than hearts and a little less convoluted than bridge.

Many of the guys listened to CDs on headsets. Rick Wise and I used the same brand of headset radio, but it was often difficult to pull in a clear signal. A few of the guys were readers, but Zac Stark was in a class by himself. That first day he was finishing up John Updike's *Rabbit Is Rich* and had Herman Hesse waiting on deck. Zac told me that he has a lot of trouble sleeping on buses—he was one of the tall guys on the team—and it was rare to see his little reading light off.

Most of our intercity trips began after a night game and distance was often measured in movies. Aberdeen to Newark, for example, was a *Braveheart* and some of the players were already planning the Nashua film festivals for the long drives to and from New Hampshire. The players bought or rented our videos and the selection was interesting. *American History X* was much better than I'd anticipated, for example, and I'm not sure that I would have seen *Booty Call* under any other circumstances.

The decision on what picture to watch when, however, was left up to the manager, who also had the option to select none of the above. There was an unwritten rule that the VCR was off-limits after a loss, when the players were supposed to contemplate their failings. Anybody who seemed to be having too good a time after a defeat would attract a withering stare from the front of the bus. Even though baseball involves more losing than any other sport—the very best teams lose at least a third of the time—losing can never be allowed to appear acceptable. After especially tough losses, the silence could be oppressive. Bad enough if you're only driving back to the hotel, stifling if you face hours on the interstate.

"That," said Danny Perez, "is why you *always* want to win on travel day."

Danny sat in the seat behind mine all season long. He's bright and when he wants to charm, which is often, his smile animates the mask he's developed to maintain his distance. Some of his teammates took this as standoffish and I guess it was. Though he often took a spot in the card game, Danny was a loner. He told me that he didn't want to get too close, that you never knew how long somebody would stay. The Spanish-speaking players formed a clique based on language and culture, but Danny wasn't part of it. I don't remember hearing him speak Spanish all year, and Danny did like to talk: about the movie on the VCR, about the route the bus driver was taking, about politics, food, history or anything else that came up.

From a distance, Danny resembles superstar catcher Mike Piazza. They share the same general body shape, flowing black hair and the blue-black cross-hatching of heavy beards on their lantern jaws. Up close, you realize that Danny is quite a bit smaller. Unlike a lot of ballplayers, Danny doesn't fudge his age, height or weight (29, 5′9″, 175 lbs) and makes no attempt to disguise his profound interest in his personal achievements. Most players can tell you exactly what they need to do to reach significant goals; for example, how many consecutive hits would elevate a batting average over .300. To speak of this openly, however, invites unpleasant and corrosive charges of selfishness. Players despise teammates who put individual success ahead of the group's, so even the greediest publicly profess the "no 'I' in 'team'" dogma. Of course, what guys do is vastly more important than what they say. Over 140 games, players cannot hide their characters. Between the lines, Danny did the right thing.

He was also one of the best interviews on the club, so good that I had to ration his appearances on the pregame show. Over the course of the season, he proved to be the most entertaining player to watch, as well.

A couple of other guys might have been faster, but none had his instinct for the ball. Some center fielders dive for balls in the gaps and make spectacular tumbling catches. The best, like Danny, make it look easy. You look up, and they're there. Despite an unfortunate habit of chasing high fastballs, he was one of the better offensive players in the league, too, a line-drive hitter with decent power and a smart, daring base runner who could bunt for a base hit or steal a base when the team needed it. During the middle of the season, he went on a tear that was simply awesome.

He hit one shot in Newark that I will never forget. The Bears' Riverfront Stadium has an exceptionally short left field and the park's design incorporates a tall chain-link fence to keep home-run balls from bouncing amid the traffic on McCarter Highway, the road that runs between the ballpark and the Passaic River. This season the Bears signed an exceptional slugger, Ozzie Canseco, twin brother of the famous major leaguer Jose Canseco, and they constructed an even taller fence, a separate structure whose mesh rose high above the old screen to soar fifty feet over the back wall of the bullpen. It was immediately dubbed the "Ozzie screen." A pop fly homer into Riverfront's bullpen was almost an embarrassment, a drive into the lower screen was legit, but one into the Ozzie screen was Ruthian.

One Sunday afternoon, Danny turned on a pitch and blasted a ball that was still rising when it lasered into the Ozzie screen two feet from the top. As I mentioned, Danny is not a guy who hits a lot of home runs, but I don't believe I've seen anyone hit a ball harder in any league. Danny Perez can play. He had just the proverbial cup of coffee in the major leagues, four games for the Milwaukee Brewers in 1996. They should have been the first four games of a big-league career.

Except Danny Perez screwed up.

"A lot of making it," Danny said, "is desire. That's true whether you're in high school or college or the pros, but in pro ball especially. When you get there, everybody's good and there are some who are just phenomenal. There are some guys who make it, they have the heart and the desire, they'll do whatever it takes. Then there are guys with ability who lost focus, who strayed. Like me. And that's why a lot of us end up here."

Danny grew up in El Paso, Texas. His mother is food services director for the school district and his father retired after thirty-five years with Greybar Electric, the last few in middle management. He calls his dad his hero and role model. "I can't remember not playing. There are pictures of me and my brother with those big red plastic bats my dad must have bought for us. We played something every season, football, basketball, baseball." It's an athletic family, with a great-uncle in Mexico's Hall of Fame and a couple of cousins who played ball in college and the minors.

Danny was the first of several players to tell me that his older brother was a much better ballplayer. "Dave is one of the top three hitters I've ever seen. Everything always came easy to him. He hit .696 in his junior year of high school. At the time, that was one of the top ten batting averages in high school ever, but he lost focus and became academically ineligible." Danny was two years younger but played on the varsity with the brother he idolized. "I didn't talk to him for two years afterward. I thought he'd let me down. The other kids at school, on the team, they didn't take it as hard as I did. I was a kid, and I didn't know." Dave Perez came out of what his brother described as a downward spiral and refocused on academics. He's now a math teacher in El Paso, married, with two kids.

Danny says the difference between them is that he always had the fire to be the best. "I was scouted by Oklahoma State, which is a very good baseball school, and by Stanford. Stanford eventually said I didn't have the academic standing, but that really wasn't it. They were also trying to get Jeffrey Hammonds at the same time [Hammonds would go on to be a regular in the majors], and they weren't sure that he wouldn't turn pro out of high school. I was their insurance. Even then," Danny added, "it's politics, it's a numbers game. He decided to go to Stanford, so I went to Oklahoma State. It turned out that we went to the College World Series and they didn't, and I was happy about that."

Danny had an academic crisis of his own at OSU, where, he admits, he didn't take his studies too seriously. He flunked out after his sophomore year and was required to graduate from a junior college in order to be eligible to play ball at OSU again. "I got a 3.7 at El Paso CC. School was all I did, study and work out. It was a turning point. I could have stalled right there. But it's a crazy world. After I got through it, I could have gone to school anywhere I wanted. I was offered a free ride at Arizona State, but I had respect for my coach at OSU. I felt I'd let him down, let my parents down and myself, too. I wanted to prove myself, so I went back there as a nonscholarship student. And my game took off."

Selected by the Milwaukee Brewers in the twenty-first round of the 1992 draft, Danny started the climb through the minors. Like a lot of college players, he skipped the lowest level of rookie ball and his first stop was Helena, Montana, in the Pioneer League. He moved up to Beloit, Wisconsin, and the Midwest League, Stockton in the California League and, in 1994, he posted a spectacular season in Double A, where the Brewers' affiliate just happened to be in El Paso. "It was the best time of my life. I was twenty-three years old, I was the local kid who made good in his hometown and it was as important to me to play off the field as well as on." Once, on the bus, we were watching a videotape that had a trailer for a football movie and there was a shot of a cheerleader asking a player to autograph her chest. "Oh, I remember those days," Danny smiled. "They'd want you to sign their tits or their ass. And I *always* had a Sharpie.

"I thought I was invincible. There are a lot of guys like that, young guys, and it catches up with you. Maybe not right away, but you break curfew often enough and you start to get a little slower." A shoulder injury cost him the entire 1995 season, but he started '96 at Triple A, in New Orleans, one rung below the majors. "I did really bad. I had a hard time recovering after a year off and my manager was really getting inside my head. I knew I had the ability, but I let outside things distract me. My manager, yes, and New Orleans, too.

"After six weeks, they called me in and told me I was being sent down to Double A. At that point, I expected the demotion. I just wanted to get away. I got off the plane in El Paso, and my dad picked me up at the airport, and I couldn't stop crying. I felt I'd let him down, let them all down. My dad is a great man and he told me I just needed to stay with it. And my manager in Double A saved me, Dave Machemer. He got me to relax and I started to hit."

He was back up in Triple A for a week when one of the big club's outfielders, Pat Listach, got hurt. As it happened, Milwaukee's general manager, Sal Bando, was in New Orleans and told Danny there was a possibility he would be called up. "We were changing planes in Chicago and I was either going to go on to Des Moines or switch to a flight to Toronto. So I found out at O'Hare that I was going to the big leagues. I only had a couple of minutes to make the flight, but I called my dad at work and he thought I was kidding. That was the high point of my career, right there. 'We did it,' he said. 'It was all worth it.'" After he hung up the phone, Danny raced for the plane to Toronto and burst through an especially well lit section of the concourse. A movie crew was filming a scene for *My Best Friend's Wedding*. "'Hey,' somebody yelled, 'where do you think you're going?' 'I'm going to the major leagues!'"

Danny joined the big club for a three-game set in Toronto and traveled with the team to Yankee Stadium in New York. "My only start was the Fourth of July against Andy Pettitte, that was really a thrill, to run onto the field there and hear my name announced by Bob Sheppard when I came up to bat. I wasn't nervous, really, not nervous playing the big leagues, but I'd been sitting for six days and knew my timing was off. [Brewers manager] Phil Garner told me I'd be playing against lefties, but we hadn't seen any until Pettitte. My parents flew up to watch me play the next game, there was another left-hander going, but Garner started Greg Vaughn in center instead. Greg Vaughn! [Vaughn was a good hitter but no center fielder.] I was pretty pissed about that, it was very disappointing.

"Listach was still on the disabled list, but they had the three-day All-Star break coming up, and he was eligible to return two days after that, and they didn't want to pay me the extra days. That's how cheap Milwaukee was."

Danny's official major league statistics show that he appeared in four games and got to bat four times without a base hit, a walk or a strikeout. It was, he says now, a very bitter cup of coffee.

"Of course, at the time, I thought I'd be headed right back up. Then, four days later in Louisville, I was arrested. I went to a place, a club, two blocks from the team hotel, and I was frustrated with myself, and I'm just at the point of asking myself, what am I doing here? And you know, the funny thing is that I think I had just figured it out. I wasn't drinking, but I was still very frustrated, I'd been there maybe twenty minutes and I went outside and pissed off an officer." This came after a night game, which means it probably happened around midnight, a time when cops are often interested in rolling up the sidewalks and ballplayers are still jazzed.

" 'What's your problem,' the officer says, and we got into an argument. A bunch of other cops start to come around, and I explain who I was and start to apologize, but I had cotton mouth and I had to spit. My spit hit the cop's shoe, and that was that. I was charged with disorderly behavior, being belligerent, drunk, assaulting an officer and resisting arrest." He hired a lawyer, who convinced the authorities to drop all the charges except for disorderly behavior, and Danny concedes that that one was justified: "I talked back."

It is entirely possible that this is a sanitized version of what happened. In any case, the Brewers responded with a ten-day suspension. They took Danny off their 40-man roster, the official list of a team's most prized players, and placed him on waivers, which meant he could be claimed by any other team that wanted him. None did.

"That was the end of my career, right there, that moment. I stayed with New Orleans for the rest of the year, but I knew in my heart that I was done. It was my worst year. I figured I'd be traded or more likely released over the winter, but that didn't happen until two weeks before spring training, when there was no time to hook up with another team. I think they did that for a reason. I was blackballed. I know I didn't turn out the way they'd hoped, but whatever they told other baseball people about me was really bad. Nobody would touch me."

When I met Danny, he said he was much more laid-back than he used to be. Even so, he was intensely competitive, cocky, sometimes abrasive and a bit of a show-off. It's not hard to see how, five years earlier, the front office of the Milwaukee Brewers might have regarded him as a total pain in the ass.

The willingness of professional sports teams to overlook behavior far worse than whatever Danny might have done is well documented, but that's for phenoms. Superstars. Danny was a twenty-first-round draft pick, so the club didn't have a large financial investment in him. He was a speedy center fielder with a good glove and an okay arm who hit for average, but not for power. An objective evaluation probably projected him as a major leaguer, but as a fourth or fifth outfielder, a late-inning defensive replacement, a pinch runner and emergency standby. His attitude might have convinced the club that he didn't have the composure to accept that role, and nobody wants utility players who are a pain in the ass. As good as Danny was and is, there are other guys in every organization more or less as good who will smile and say "Yes, sir."

Danny was devastated after he was released by the Brewers in the spring of 1997. "If I'm not allowed to play, okay, I'm smart, there are other things I can do, I have other things going for me, but it was so hard to swallow that I couldn't play." In March, he got a call from the Northern League, the oldest and best known of the independent leagues; it was where slugger Darryl Strawberry went to play after a celebrated stint in a drug rehabilitation center. "Now, I had vowed to retire before I'd ever play in an independent league, but it was tough to do that. It was a chance to play. I knew Strawberry had played in the league the year before, that gave it some credibility, so I went to play for Sioux City, the Sioux City Explorers. They had an informal agreement of some kind with the Arizona Diamondbacks, that's what I heard, anyway, so I figured I'd be back in a real organization in half a season. I hit .410 over the first couple of months, and nothing happened. That's when I knew that whatever Milwaukee had said, the word on me had spread. And I gave up.

"The Fourth of July hit me very hard that season. I was a year away from the major leagues. I was on bad terms with my dad, who was disappointed with me. I was still twenty-five, still young and headstrong."

Danny met his future wife, Kim, that season and credits her with getting him through it. Once it was over, he moved to Florida to be with her, got a job selling shoes at The Sports Authority and thought about how he could finish up the degree he'd started at Oklahoma State. By which time it was spring again. His old El Paso manager, Dave Machemer, got him a tryout with the Baltimore Orioles organization and he went north with the Bowie Baysox, back in Double A. In '98 I was the second banana in the Baysox radio booth, but I missed the start of the season on an extended assignment for NPR's *Radio Expeditions*. By the time I got back, Danny was already gone. "There's no excuse, I just didn't play well."

Back in Florida, Danny got a call from Wayne Krenchiki, manager of the Black Diamonds, a team in the brand-new Atlantic League that was then playing in Newburgh, New York. "I figured the shot with Baltimore was my last chance, but I was engaged and I needed the money, and, yeah, part of it was the bullshit job down in Florida. Plus I wanted to lose some of the taste of playing like crap.

"The conditions in Newburgh were horrible, we all lived in a dormitory with no air-conditioning and the field was bad, but Kim came up to see me play and I did well. I had a good time. I was surprised by the level of play, too. This was a good league in '98, probably equivalent to Double A, and it's gotten better. There were a lot of factors, but I never thought I would get back with an organization, back to the majors.

"At the end of the season, I retired. Officially. I got married, I had school stuff, work, regular guy stuff. Three months of that, and I knew I wanted to play again. I wanted to do well and have fun and make money, and it was the lifestyle I knew. I wasn't a regular Joe who went to college and got a job. I thought if I was playing, I could get experience in baseball operations, learn to work in the front office of an organization, make some contacts. I knew it would affect my marriage, but Kim was all for it. I didn't want to be away from my wife, but I decided I needed to play."

That season, 1999, the Black Diamonds were supposed to

move into a new ballpark being built in the Lehigh Valley near Easton, Pennsylvania. The owner ran out of money, though, construction stopped and the team spent the entire year on the road.

In a league where the top players get no more than $3,000 per month, the meal money they get when they're on the road is pretty important. Fifteen dollars a day isn't a lot of money, but a week's worth feels like a wad and it's cash that never has to be explained to the IRS or the wife. "The money was okay, and it was a really good group, too. There were cliques like you have on any team, but everybody hung out. I didn't go out much, I'd learned my lesson about that, but I saved some money and for a long time, we played pretty well.

"In August, though, it got tough. We got tired, and it's hard to play on the road all the time, it's a spiritual drain to wear the black hats every night. You want people to cheer you, your own fans. When you're the villains all the time, it starts to feel empty. Late in the season, we're just two games out of first place with twenty-five games left to play, and we lose twelve in a row. We just couldn't get up for the games anymore, we got worn out."

Danny was an Atlantic League All-Star that season and when Adam Gladstone left Lehigh Valley's front office, he figured out a way to bring him along as one of the cornerstones of the new team in Aberdeen. "I trust Adam and I look forward to being associated with the Ripken name, that means a lot in baseball. Plus there's an opportunity to work for the team in the front office in the off-season, so I'm excited about this year."

The decision to play the 2000 season, though, came at the price of divorce. "When I was with her, Kim was the one making the money. I need to learn how to be independent and establish myself, so I can be an equal partner. I didn't have that with Kim in Florida. She's a great woman, so if I can establish myself, maybe I'd like to get back with her. I also knew that if I was going to play, I'd want to have sex with other women, and I didn't want to do that while I was married. Besides, there's the adrenaline. Before every game, I get butterflies before my first at-bat. That's what tells me I still want to play."

ATLANTIC LEAGUE STANDINGS						
THROUGH GAMES OF MAY 7						
NORTH DIVISION	**W**	**L**	**PCT.**	**GB**	**STREAK**	**LAST 10**
Nashua	8	2	.800	—	W 5	8–2
Long Island	4	5	.444	3.5	L 3	4–5
Bridgeport	4	5	.444	3.5	W 1	4–5
Newark	3	6	.333	4.5	L 1	3–6
SOUTH DIVISION						
Lehigh Valley	6	3	.667	—	L 2	6–3
Aberdeen	5	4	.556	1.0	W 2	5–4
Somerset	4	6	.400	2.5	W 1	4–5
Atlantic City	3	6	.333	3.0	L 1	3–6

*T*he bats arrived in long, rectangular boxes addressed to manager Darrell Evans. With the major league All-Star Game in Atlanta this year, the annual slugging contest would feature some of the host team's old favorites, and Darrell was one of the ex-Braves selected for the honor. This is not the Home Run Derby, a prime-time celebration of today's great hitters, but a newer, made-for-cable-TV event where old-timers lead teams that include celebrities. There's a complicated scoring system that assigns ten points, say, for a drive just past second base and thirty for a fly ball to the warning track, but Darrell couldn't have cared less about that. He was going to Atlanta to hit a dinger.

There were three special bats in each of the two cardboard boxes, half of them black, the others a deep, burnished burgundy, all with Darrell's name and the event spelled out in gold lettering. As he pulled them out of their individual sleeves of bubble wrap, the lacquer was so shiny they almost seemed wet. I figured they were presentation bats, destined for an autograph, a charity auction and a collector's case, but Darrell picked out a black one and stepped into the batting cage.

Darrell Evans might have added an inch or two to his waistline since he last played in 1989, but he closely resembled the slugger who menaced big-league pitchers for twenty-one years. He's a big man, 6′2″, with a dark complexion and short black hair, the Indian side of his heritage evident in wide, prominent cheekbones. His batting stance was unchanged: relaxed, feet spread slightly wider than his shoulders, no gimmicks. He took a couple of practice cuts, signaled that he was ready, flexed his knees, cocked his hands low, leaned back, lifted the heel of his front foot and then stepped forward to meet the pitch in one smooth motion.

"Dammit."

He didn't even glance at the fly ball he'd lofted fairly deep to right. He knew he hadn't gotten it from the feel. The next pitch he fouled straight back. It rattled off the chain link of the batting cage and spun back toward home plate. He reached out with his gorgeous new bat and flicked it out of the way.

"C'mon, now."

The sound this time was unmistakable, a clean, crisp, satisfying thwack. The line drive was over the fence and gone in a blink.

"*There* you go."

"Dang!"

"That the best you can do, Skip?"

The banter bubbled as Darrell gave up his spot and stepped around to the side of the cage to examine the damage. Several guys gathered and Darrell passed the bat around so that each could look at the scar along the edge and the slightly flattened dent on the sweet spot.

"So," somebody asked, "what did you think?"

"Not bad. Good balance. Pretty nice."

Tyrone Horne wrapped his hands around the handle and held the bat out to gauge the heft. He glanced up at the manager. "You mind?"

"Help yourself."

Tyrone carefully placed his own bat next to the cage and stepped in to take his cuts with Darrell's black beauty.

Bats were a constant topic of conversation around the cage. The team supplied Louisville Sluggers in a few standard sizes, which were inevitably too long or too heavy or too something. Gil Martinez cut the ends off to make his lighter and Danny Perez, the contrarian, insisted that they should have bought Rawlings bats instead.

"They're harder. Better wood." And maybe a dollar more expensive apiece, which was why Danny figured he was stuck with inferior lumber for the season. All the manufacturers save their very best wood for the big-leaguers, anyway, so just about everybody else had to settle for second-rate stock. A few players bought their own bats. Randy Brown, the shortstop of the Somerset Patriots, had his own personalized models—Gil got one from him and stained it orange so he wouldn't lose track of it. That was his heavy bat. The cut-down Louisville Sluggers were his light bats and those he painted blue.

Tyrone Horne brought two big boxes of white bats with him when he came to play with Aberdeen a few weeks after the season started. The color was very unusual and when I first saw them, I thought they were painted, too, but up close, you could see the whorls of the wood grain. Tyrone said this was the natural shade of specially selected white ash. He belted a couple of shots with Darrell's black bat, handed it back with a murmur of appreciation and walked over to the side of the cage where he'd left his own. He picked up the white bat and cradled it.

"Don't you worry, baby," he said softly. "You're still my favorite."

I thought Darrell took regular BP so that he wouldn't embarrass himself when his turn to hit came up in Atlanta, but I was wrong. He batted every day because that's who he was, and he wasn't worried about looking bad, he was out to show he could still hit with anybody. He'd never say that in Atlanta, of course. When he got to Turner Field, he'd say that he'd taken a couple of swings to get ready, nothing special.

Part of the reason was the bitterness he still felt about the end of his playing career. After the 1988 season, his twentieth in the big leagues, he was released by the Detroit Tigers. "They said I was too old, that my bat was slowing down."

The record book suggests that they may have had a point: Darrell batted .208 for the Tigers that year. "The hell with that," he told me. "I led the team in homers, I was second on the club in RBIs, I'm one of the most productive guys in the lineup and they tell me I can't hit anymore." He'd been one of a group of older players who won the World Series for Detroit in 1984, but, after contending for a few more years, the club had faded a bit and management decided it was time to rebuild. Darrell couldn't see it then, and doesn't agree with it now. Those tough old guys had a run or two left, he argues, and, besides, what was the rush? The kids the Tigers brought up didn't turn out so well. The team hasn't contended since.

In 1989 Darrell finished up with his original club in Atlanta. Because the National League plays without the designated hitter, he was limited to part-time duty, and he still cranked out 11 homers. That made it 414 in all, a total that put him in illustrious company. He is one of only two men to have a 40-home-run season in both major leagues, the oldest ever to win a home-run title, and he piled up impressive career numbers of runs, RBIs and walks. A .248 lifetime batting average prevented any serious consideration for the Hall of Fame, but by any measure, Darrell Evans was one of the premier sluggers of his day.

"I always wanted to be a manager when I got out. As a player, I really enjoyed, you know, second-guessing my managers, and"—he laughed—"I guess a couple of them knew that, too. But I got a hitting-coach deal right away, a major league job with the Yankees, and that's the track I sort of ended up on. I really enjoyed it. It's a lot of fun to work with the hitters and get people better, but the one thing about the hitting-coach job is that, once the game starts, your job is ended. You can talk to them a little bit, but most hitters don't want too much going on during a game. As a manager, well, that's when the fun starts. You have to make all sorts of quick decisions. There are so many variables out there, it really keeps you on your toes. Four years ago, I finally just said, I'm not going to be a hitting guy anymore, I want to be a manager."

To prove himself, he took a job as the skipper of the Tyler Wildcatters of the Texas-Louisiana League, an independent circuit several cuts below the Atlantic League. In 1998 he managed the Wilmington Blue Rocks of the South Atlantic League—A ball—and last year, he moved up to run the Milwaukee Brewers' Double A affiliate, the Huntsville Stars. Darrell's coaching staff at Aberdeen included another long-time major leaguer, pitching coach Rick Wise, and Dan DiPace, who played many years in the minors.

Aside from a little gray and a few facial crinkles, Rick Wise looked lean and ready to play. His long big-league career started with a lowlight: as a rookie, he was on the Phillies team that gave away a huge lead and blew the National League pennant in 1964. Later, he pitched a no-hit game against Cincinnati when they were the Big Red Machine, was one of the principals in a gigantic trade that sent him to Saint Louis in return for the great Steve Carlton, and got swapped again in another huge deal to Boston. He had probably his best year in 1975. Coming off a shoulder injury, he won 19 games for the Red Sox in the regular season, another in the American League playoffs against Oakland, and one more in the World Series—the classic Game Six that ended with Carlton Fisk's dramatic home run. Rick could hit a little, too. He had two homers in that no-hitter.

Dan DiPace looked less like an old ballplayer and more like a guy who once ran a bar and restaurant. He was originally drafted by the Los Angeles Dodgers in 1963, but, much to his regret, they left him unprotected in a minor league draft and he was taken by the Minnesota Twins. He had some good years—in 1965 he was the MVP of the Midwest League—but the Twins were a powerhouse in those years and Dan was buried in the organization. His best shot at the majors came in

1968, when the Twins traded him to the hapless Washington Senators, but the deal was nullified when the other guy failed his physical examination. The Twins finally cut him in 1970, and he decided to go into the family business. For fifteen years he owned and operated Danny's Club Lounge, near the railroad station in Scarsdale, New York, selling drinks to men loosening their ties on their way home from Wall Street and Madison Avenue.

Dan got back into baseball as a part-time scout after he sold the bar and moved to Florida. His son Danny was a ballplayer, too, a first baseman–outfielder who played for Darrell in Huntsville. Dan and Darrell got to know each other and when Darrell offered him a job with Aberdeen, Dan jumped at the chance to get back into uniform. He spoke quickly and often and couldn't hide his emotions. Unlike Darrell, who was fairly even-tempered, Dan was ebullient when things went well and morose when they didn't. He coached first base, but his actual job didn't have a title; manager's friend was as good a description as any, or perhaps consigliere. Where Darrell was a cautious tactician who trusted his hitters, played for the big inning and hated to give away outs, Dan loved "little ball," the game of bunts and hit-and-run plays. Both styles reflected what they'd done well as players.

"Oh, I could hit," Dan told me in the bar one night. "I couldn't hit 'em like he did," nudging Darrell, "I was a line-drive hitter and I could run in those days, I had good speed."

"Frickin' Judy," Darrell pronounced with mock contempt. "Duck snorts and little slap hits the other way." "Judy," from Punch and Judy, was a slugger's slur for a singles hitter.

"I had gap power," Dan replied indignantly.

"Gap power, my ass. Guy says he's got gap power, means he ran out a couple of bloop doubles."

"At least I could run. You figure you'd hurt yourself if you tried to leg out a few?"

"Hey, when I hit 'em, I could run just as fast or as slow as I wanted."

I played the audience for this double act all summer long, listening to stories about Rico Carty and Dick Drago, what buses were like in the old Provincial League, and how missing the cutoff man changed the course of the seventh inning.

Both of them loved to steal the opposing team's signs. Early in the season, on our first trip in to play the Long Island Ducks, this became a little obvious. Every time a Duck runner tried to steal second base, Darrell called for a pitchout. The Arsenal pitcher threw the next one in deliberately high and outside, giving the catcher an easy throw to catch the would-be thief. After five of these in succession, I spoke up after the game and told Darrell that he might want to guess wrong every once in a while.

"Hey, Dan," he said playfully, "he's not as dumb as we thought."

For the rest of the season, Darrell blamed me every time a pitchout didn't work: "Just following your advice, don't want 'em knowing we can read their signs."

Another time, after a horrendous error led to a miserable loss, I recalled Darrell's remark that seemed to characterize independent-league players—there was a reason they were all here.

"That's true," Darrell said. He thought for a moment and went on: "But you know, there are reasons all of 'em shouldn't be here, too. There's not all that much difference between these guys and the major leagues. I mean, I've seen some rookie league games in this league and I guess tonight was one of them, but you see those in the majors, too, just not so often.

This game is so hard, but these guys have talent, they can do some things. A break here or there, who knows."

One of Tyrone Horne's bats is in Cooperstown. In 1998 Tyrone did something unprecedented: he homered for the cycle. Hitting for the cycle is unusual; once a year or so, somebody will get a single, double, triple and home run in the same game. Four homers in a game is much rarer, and, so far as anyone knows, Tyrone is the only professional ballplayer ever to hit a solo shot, a two-run job, a three-run homer and a grand slam in the same game.

"I did it in my first four times up," he told me. "I came up again in the eighth and I was going for five, but I missed it."

Tyrone has worked hard to overcome a stutter and, like a lot of people with a speech defect, tends to keep quiet. He is a fireplug of a man, only 5´8″ or so, but muscled as impressively as any ballplayer I've seen. With a "lady" in his hands, he is a vision of balance and grace. Outside the batter's box, he lumbers. Good outfielders, like Danny Perez, run on the balls of their feet and seem to glide across the grass. Tyrone runs on his heels, and the ground shakes beneath him. He doesn't have the height and agility to play first base, and he can't run or throw well enough to play the outfield.

In 1998 the St. Louis Cardinals hired this professional hitter to protect their big prospect, number-one draft pick J. D. Drew. The idea was to make sure Drew saw a lot of pitches to hit. If Lou Gehrig is batting fourth in the lineup, Babe Ruth, hitting third, will get a lot of fat pitches. Batting behind Drew for the Arkansas Travelers of the Double A Texas League, Tyrone had a fabulous season. In addition to his unique home-run binge, he batted .312 with 139 runs batted in and a total of 37 homers in just 123 games. He won the league's MVP

Award by acclamation. After the season, J. D. Drew was promoted to Triple A, on the fast track to the big time. Tyrone
Horne was picked up by the Phillies, who sent him to Reading
in the Double A Eastern League to protect *their* number-one
draft pick, Pat Burrell.

"What do I have to do?" Tyrone asked. "How come I have
a better year than the number-one draft pick, but he's a
prospect and I'm not?"

Tyrone's age and defensive deficiencies were part of the reason, but money is a big part of it, too. J. D. Drew and Pat
Burrell signed multimillion-dollar deals, and the executives
who recommended those huge bonuses made sure they got
every opportunity. Tyrone Horne was a forty-fourth-round
draft pick, a minor league free agent without a position. No
player development director's job rode on his success. By 2000
both Drew and Burrell were in the major leagues. Tyrone
Horne would hit his way out of Aberdeen and the Atlantic
League, but only as far as Double A.

Johnny Isom used to be a prospect. Physically, he's a bigger,
right-handed version of Tyrone Horne. In his case, the line-
backer's body came with decent speed and a strong arm, but
where Tyrone's swing is short and sweet and simple, Johnny
fights himself. His first and most serious problem is that he
bails out. Instead of striding straight back toward the mound
as he swings, his front foot lurches toward third base. Many in
baseball regard stepping into the bucket more as a moral failure than a mechanical flaw, an admission of fear. When I first
saw Johnny hit in 1997 with the Bowie Baysox, this tendency
meant that right-handed pitchers could get him to lunge at
balls on the outside edge of the plate; but he punished them if
they missed and he was absolute murder on lefties. He tied the
club record for runs batted in that season, and seemed to be on

course to assume a spot as a middle-of-the order masher in Baltimore.

As one batting coach after another tried to correct his stride, Johnny regressed. Trying to keep his front shoulder in, he started to drop it. Setting himself to hit the outside pitch, he tied himself up inside. Three years later you could almost hear him listening to all the different bits of advice as the pitch came in. He couldn't even hit lefties anymore.

By contrast, Alex Andreopoulos should have been a hot commodity: a young, left-handed-hitting catcher with out-standing defensive skills and more than a little pop in his bat. Alex grew up speaking Greek at home and in his neighbor-hood in Toronto, and his English was colored by both Greek and Canadian accents. He went to college at Seton Hall University, a baseball powerhouse, and after moving swiftly up the minor league ladder, this season Andro expected to be a major league backup with the Brewers or, at worst, one of those guys who shuttle between the Triple A squad and the major league team. Over the winter, though, Milwaukee fired its manager and purged the front office. The executives who'd drafted Alex and had a stake in his career were gone. The new regime brought in some guys they liked better and offered Alex a ticket back to Double A. Insulted, he came to Aberdeen to audition for all the major league organizations.

David Steed might have been the guy the Atlantic League was created for. From Mississippi—his accent was stronger, though softer, than Andro's—Steeder had spent the previous three years in the Dodgers' Triple A team in Albuquerque, but played less and less each season. He was a backup catcher and sometime first baseman, the kind of player organizations use to fill out their minor league rosters. Hitting infrequently, his average dropped to .210 and when L.A. released him, there wasn't a lot on his stat sheet to interest anyone else. Newly married with a kid on the way, Steed came to the Atlantic League to give the game one more shot.

He wanted a spot where he could catch every day and show what he could do, and he should have stuck to his plan. Dan DiPace spotted him belting line drives in spring training, and when the Arsenal acquired the more accomplished Andreopoulos to catch, Steed amiably agreed to learn to play third base. Behind the plate he was smooth, sure-handed and strong-armed. At third he was a statue with hands of stone. Steed never let his fielding problems affect his bat, though, and he was the second-biggest surprise hitting star of the early season.

Gil Martinez was number one. Gil spent three unhappy years in the Boston Red Sox organization in the late eighties then went back home to Puerto Rico. "I just didn't want to play no more." He switched from baseball to fast-pitch softball, and eventually played for the Puerto Rican national team in the Pan American Games. "They throw a riser there, you don't see that in baseball, that's a tough pitch to hit. They throw hard, too, and from forty-five feet away. You got to have a quick bat." After nine years, a friend suggested the Atlantic League as an opportunity to make some money playing ball in the summertime. In 1999 he played part time for the Somerset Patriots and hit what they assumed was a fluky .309. They let him go in the league's expansion draft.

The Arsenal didn't have time to stitch the players' names on the backs of their uniforms for the opening home stand and when the team returned from the first road trip, the players eagerly examined their home whites. The lettering on Gil's number 12 read "Martienz." He decided to embrace it. "That Polish kid can hit," he said, "and he can steal a base for you, too." In fact, he was thrown out stealing as often as he succeeded, but he could most definitely hit. Gil started off 24 for his first 50, was the league's Player of the Month in May and, in sweet vindication, went to the All-Star Game in Somerset with more votes than any other outfielder in the South Division.

"Martienz" was the leader, but almost everybody hit well in May. The Arsenal's team batting average was well over .300. The gaudy stats were partly attributable to the cozy dimensions of Thomas Run Park, but Darrell could take some of the credit. He seemed to be most comfortable with his elbows resting on the bar halfway up the back of the batting cage, calling out tips and encouragement as his team took BP. In fact, he spent so much time working with the hitters that I sometimes wondered if he'd really given up on the coaching track.

The entire season was a tutorial in hitting. Early one afternoon I found the professor perched on a stool on the edge of the infield grass in front of home plate. Protected by a portable chain-link screen, he flipped baseballs toward his students and kept up a running commentary.

"Move up to the plate a bit, that's the way, it'll bring the ball inside to you. You want to see the ball inside, that's where you want to hit it, look for the ball inside and below the belt, that's the one you want. Take your best swing every time. If you look for the ball there, it'll be there for you. Position yourself right, and every pitch looks the same, no matter where it is."

He cocks the ball in his right hand, as if ready to throw overhand.

"From here, you have less time to react than in a game, this is quicker than a game." He switches to an underhand delivery and flips the ball across the plate. "Short and quick. If you're short and quick, he can't beat you inside. You've seen me hit the ball, and most of the time I pull it. That's not because I want to pull it, that's a product of being short and quick. Keep your hands inside the ball, get the head of the bat out—no, no, no!" Darrell interrupts himself as big Erskine Kelley stretches his long arms to take a big swing at a ball outside and sends a lazy fly to right. "Don't reach for it! If the hands are that far out from the body, the swing is longer and slower. Kelley, show me that swing again." He gets up from the stool, walks around the screen to stand next to the big right-handed hitter. "Okay, stop it there. See? When you extend like that, the bat is angled back as it comes through the hitting zone. There's less hitting surface, and you can see why he hit that little dunker to right, the bat's angled that way. You don't want that bat tilted, and you sure don't want a slow swing.

"Now, Sarge," he said, using Kelley's nickname, "try it again, but keep your hands in, short and quick. That's it." Darrell stopped the swing with the bat over the plate. "Now the bat's horizontal as it comes through the zone, see? If you're short and quick, you don't have to reach for that ball outside. Move up closer, be quick, get your hands out in front and the bat will go to the outside corner and get it." He moves back to the stool, flips a ball to the exact spot, and Kelley kills it. "You see how everything's together now? The bat is so much faster, he can't get it past you. That ball was away, and you smoked it over the lights. Remember"—this time he held two balls in his hand—"there's only this much difference between the outside corner and down the middle. So if it's a strike, if it's in my zone, other than that I don't care where it is, I'm just going to hit it. If it goes that way"—he shrugs toward right, the opposite field for a right-handed hitter like Kelley—"that's fine. It's going to go that way 'cause maybe it gets a little deeper on me, that's all, but if I hit it perfect, I can drive the crap out of it."

I wondered if Darrell's philosophy wasn't just a slugger's creed.

"It's different from what everybody else preaches," Tim Lindycamp tells me as we stand behind the cage and watch the lesson, "but I think it's a better philosophy of hitting." Lindycamp coaches the baseball team at Harford Community College and took the presence of professional interlopers as an opportunity to enroll in the Evans Baseball Academy. A slight, sandy-haired man, Tim spent most of his time with the Arsenal after school let out and became a convert.

"A lot of people teach that on the curveball outside, they want you to drive that ball to right field." (This is based on a right-handed hitter.) "The same thing with the fastball outside, take it to right. To do that, they say, you should let the ball get past you a little bit, so your bat's basically at a forty-five-degree angle when you hit it."

"This is what they call an inside-out swing?"

"Exactly. But if you have quick hands and you can pick up that it's going to be an outside pitch, you can still get your hands out and drive that ball up the middle or even pull it. You have more bat surface to hit with."

"I can see why that might be better for power hitters, but is it better for singles hitters, too? I mean, the first lesson I learned was 'Take two and hit to right.'"

Tim laughs. From that alone, he could have guessed that I batted ninth for the Coffin Pump Pirates when I was a kid. "I don't know how quick your hands were in Little League," he says, "but, yes, I think this is better all around. If you have somebody out there throwing 90 miles an hour, and you're trying to hit the ball once it's past you, your chances aren't very good. If I can get to that same 90-mile-an-hour fastball while it's out in front of me, then all I have to do is adjust my hands and I can be more successful."

The one guy who didn't start well was Danny Perez. He twisted a knee in spring training and sat out the first few games of the season. Overeager, he tried to come back too soon and hurt it again. By the time he was healthy enough to play, he was so anxious that he started to think too much. Thinking, he explained, is no good for a hitter. The first few balls he hit hard all seemed to find the other team's gloves.

"Now, that happens enough times, you start thinking, 'I'm getting into a slump,' and it starts playing with your head a little bit. Pretty soon, I'm not hitting balls at people, I'm not hitting them at all, so you think, 'Oh, no. here we go.'"

Modern technology contributes to the problem. Most of the ballparks in the Atlantic League have whiz-bang scoreboards that show the hitter's picture and recompute his batting average every time he comes up. Danny stood at home plate and watched his average sink below .200. In minor league parks, where the crowds are so close, he could hear the fans dismiss him as an easy out. "It's so social when you're a player, people see your mistakes, but that's part of the game and you have to deal with it mentally."

Just as a lot of guys will do things exactly the same way when they're in a hot streak—wear the same socks every day or eat the same pregame meal—many change their routines when they're slumping. "Yeah," Danny agrees, "guys are superstitious, but I try not to let it get into my head too much." Since he is not superstitious, Danny does exactly the opposite, changing things up when he's going well and sticking to his routines when he's slumping.

The truth behind that perverse logic is that there's nothing wrong with his swing. Last season, after all, it was good enough for a .310 average. The problem is mental and he doesn't want to compound it by tinkering with his mechanics. "You think too much, and you're going to get hurt sometimes." He listens to his manager's theories respectfully, but from a distance. He is never among those who show up early for extra hitting. "I learned a long time ago, don't volunteer for anything." Yet, when the hits finally start to come in bunches for him, he credits Darrell. "In BP one day I noticed that he holds his hands a little lower than usual. My hands have a tendency to stay at about shoulder level. I drop them to cock the bat, and sometimes I drop them too low, so I decided to hold my hands where I was going to cock, and that's allowed me to get more direct to the ball. In layman's terms, I'm a lot quicker."

I mention this to Darrell, and he glows. "In the long run," he says, "they kinda gotta teach themselves, make the adjustments on their own. When you're a young player, you want people to tell you what to do, and it may not always work for you. Just because it works for one guy, that doesn't mean it's the correct thing for you because everybody's different, they're built differently, they all have different swings, one guy's hands might be stronger, all that kinda stuff."

For a long time the Arsenal could boast three .400 hitters in their lineup, but everyone knew that couldn't last. And there were some ominous glitches in the offensive juggernaut. There were not very many homers in the blizzard of hits. This

wasn't critical as long as the club continued to pound out sin-
gles and doubles, but splurges don't last forever and in the long
run, teams that lack power have a hard time scoring. Another
ominous sign was speed, or lack thereof. Of the regulars, only
Danny Perez and Maleke Fowler could be described as fast.
Everybody else was average or below, and David Steed and
Mike Wolff were way, way below. The infield defense stunk.
Among the starting pitchers, lefty Zac Stark jumped out to a
great 5–1 record, and everyone else was inconsistent except
Miguel Garcia, the number-two starter, who was simply awful.
The bullpen, including closer Jose Alberro, was a bright spot,
but all those bad starts forced the relievers to pick up a lot of
additional innings, which wore them down.

Because the league had expanded to eight teams, it arranged
itself into two divisions for the 2000 season and Aberdeen
lucked out; the South Division was much the weaker of the
two. While the Arsenal's record wasn't good, Aberdeen
remained fairly close to first place because its divisional rivals
weren't a lot better. The schedule was balanced, 20 games
against each of the other clubs, and the league played a split
season. That meant that the teams in first place in their divisions after 70 games won a spot in the postseason playoffs and
everybody started over again from scratch. The first-half winner from each division would play off against the second-half
winner for the right to move on to the finals. If a team won
both halves, it earned a bye in the first round and went straight
on to the best-three-out-of-five championship series.

There are some important differences between the independent leagues and the affiliated minors. One is the sense of living
on the brink. Players on every level are insecure, but in the independent leagues, there's a real fear that the next injury or slump

will be the last; there is no lower rung to drop down to. Miguel Garcia, for example, was Aberdeen's best pitcher in spring training, but he told no one when his elbow started to hurt. There is a disabled list in the independent leagues and insurance to cover medical care, but teams really don't want to pay guys who can't play. Miguel kept his silence, went out to the mound every fifth day and got hammered. After four horrendous starts, Rick and Darrell finally took him out of the rotation. That's when he admitted to the injury, which was diagnosed as tendinitis. Because he'd thrown so well in the spring and because the Arsenal desperately needed pitching, he stayed with the team. After difficult weeks of rest and rehab, he returned with an outstanding appearance against the Bridgeport Bluefish. Coming on in relief in a tight game, he threw three spotless innings and finished with a flourish, popping up former big-leaguer Chico Lind on a nasty slider. As the ball settled into Mike Wolff's glove, Garcia stumbled toward the dugout, clutching his pitching arm. X-rays disclosed a stress fracture in his elbow, and he was done for the year.

Another difference is the obvious fact that independent teams are not part of an organization. When an affiliated team loses a player to injury, the organization provides a replacement, a kid promoted from a lower rung, or somebody dropping down. They may even sign an independent-league player to come in and fill the gap. A spate of injuries and promotions can leave affiliated teams depleted, but usually no longer than a few days. Aberdeen, by contrast, was short at least one player for most of the year. The same day that Miguel Garcia went down, starting pitcher Andy Bair hurt his arm as well, and it would be a week and a half before reinforcements arrived, a span of nine games where relievers had to make emergency starts and everybody threw more than they probably should have. It does not take long for added strain to burn out an already fragile pitching staff.

Another important distinction between affiliated teams and independents is the urgency to win. In organized ball, the only title that matters is the World Series. A South Atlantic League championship might be nice, but it's almost beside the point. From the organizations' point of view, the minor leagues exist solely to develop players for the parent team; winning is decidedly secondary. When he managed the Wilmington Blue Rocks, for example, Darrell cut back the playing time of a big left-handed-hitting outfield prospect. The kid couldn't hit left-handed pitching, so Darrell platooned him. The change helped the team climb into first place, but it also got Darrell fired. The big club was more interested to find out if the prospect could learn to hit lefties than it was in winning the Sallie League. Similarly, pitching prospects are often restricted to a certain number of pitches and must be taken out when they hit that total no matter what the game situation might be or whether the bullpen had been used up the day before.

Darrell believes this is profoundly unfair and shortsighted. "A lot of the time, the players who don't get signed to the big-money contracts have more heart and more instinct for the game, and those guys don't get a chance to play and develop." Prospects also start to focus on their own at-bats or their own hundred pitches and lose track of the little things that often make the difference between winning and losing. "To develop into a great player," Darrell says, "you have to go through winning and losing situations. Winning should matter, because when you get to the big leagues, it's the only thing that matters. Learning the little things should be a big part of the process, you shouldn't be going out there game after game just to get your work in. You have to teach 'em how to win. Here, we have a lot more control. It's more of a competitive situation than anywhere besides the major leagues. The emphasis is always on winning the ball game, and whoever's playing the best are the ones who give us the best chance to win, so they're the ones that are going to play."

Deconstructing the star system is much easier when everyone is paid poorly. The top salary in the Atlantic League is $3,000 per month, the minimum $850, and while there are rumors that a few big names get a little extra under the table, the limit appears pretty firm. An informal agreement caps each team's player payroll at $250,000 per season, but Bridgeport, Nashua and Somerset seemed to spend far more freely than Aberdeen and Lehigh Valley.

From a manager's point of view, it's liberating to be paid more than any of your players, to control who plays and why without the front office looking over your shoulder, to be freed from the chore of filling out detailed progress reports on each player. They, too, are all here for a reason.

For Willie Upshaw, Bridgeport is the first rung of a managerial career. Upshaw was a solid if not spectacular player for ten years in the majors, mostly with the Toronto Blue Jays. He played a couple more seasons in Japan, then spent seven years as a hitting instructor and batting coach for the Blue Jays and the Texas Rangers. Like Darrell Evans, he had to move all the way down to the independent leagues to find a team willing to give a hitting specialist the opportunity to manage. His Bluefish posted the best record in both of the Atlantic League's first two seasons, won the championship in 1999, and they did it with style. Bridgeport played crisp, disciplined, efficient baseball. Serious and well organized, Willie Upshaw is the odds-on favorite to become the first independent league manager to make it to the majors.

For Somerset, Sparky Lyle is a commodity. In the 1970s, Lyle won fame as a charter member of the New York Yankees' Bronx Zoo, as celebrated for sitting in birthday cakes as he was for his pitching, which was good enough to earn him a Cy Young Award as the best in the American League. "I never had any hopes of being back in baseball after I retired," he says. He was out of uniform for eighteen years, so baseball evidently agreed with him. The Somerset Patriots hired him for his name and they market it relentlessly. A seven-foot-tall "Sparky" mascot romps through the stands during the game, a giant blue caricature of the manager complete with trademark handlebar mustache. Smaller versions, of course, are available in the gift shop. The fact that Sparky is a poor field tactician is much less important than his success as an image. And in 1999, despite a steady stream of decisions as impulsive as his stunts with the Yankees, Sparky's players mounted an improbable late-season charge that carried the Patriots into the playoffs and won him the Manager of the Year Award.

For Darrell Evans, the Atlantic League is a refuge. This is his fourth team in as many years. He was fired halfway through his first season as a manager in affiliated ball, and his second organization did not ask him back. "I feel very fortunate to have this chance," he told me. "Heck, this is my thirty-fourth year in professional baseball. It's so great just to put a uniform on and come out here, to be around young people and pass on all the stuff I learned. This is as close to being a player as I think any other thing you can do in baseball, and I get to kinda play through the rest of the guys, but you ask, why am I here, and I guess the answer is that I don't know how to do anything else."

• • •

The All-Star break was the same week for both the Atlantic and the major leagues. Darrell left early to participate in the hitting contest in Atlanta and Bill Ripken came up to run the team for a couple of games, which both he and the players enjoyed. It was a little like a favorite uncle coming over to baby-sit who lets the kids stay up late and eat all the junk food they want. Everybody had a good time and there was no permanent damage. When he returned, Darrell said he'd had a great time seeing old friends, but he was disappointed not to get a dinger. He trashed his performance so much that I was a little surprised when I eventually saw the TV show on ESPN2; Darrell hit a couple of long line drives, but just didn't lift them.

Over the first few weeks of the season, our schedule was normal—ten home games, eight away. Because of previous commitments at Thomas Run Park, we were now about to hit the road for 26 games in 27 days. Danny Perez and some of the other guys who'd had experience with long road trips said it would test the team, but temper it, too. Thrown together every day in the same hotels and the same restaurants with little distraction, we would know a great deal more about each other after the next month.

Few of the players looked forward to the trip, but I have to confess that I did. It was a great deal easier to work on the road because the visitors' radio booths provided ample counter space to set up my equipment, power and a phone line to plug into, walls to tape up my stat sheets and, most precious of all, privacy. Once I closed the door, I could concentrate on the game without the distractions of the crowded press box at Thomas Run.

Like everyone else in sports broadcasting, I used a headset microphone that looked like a fuzzy dot on the end of a small boom that extended from my left earphone to the corner of my mouth. A separate mike clamped outside the window of the visitors' radio booth picked up the sounds of the crowd and the public address system. Slowly, I realized that the headset allowed me to stand up and move around during the broadcast, and since I was alone, I gave in to the urge for grand gesticulation. For some reason, my otherwise excellent headsets had very short cords, though, so every once in a while I would roam too far and the headset would yank me back like an overeager puppy on a leash.

I also realized another huge advantage of the road: as far as my audience was concerned, nothing happened until I said it did. At home there were always a few people in the stands with radios, but when we were in Atlantic City or Somerset, I could safely ignore a meaningless foul ball or another throw over to first base until I'd finished my anecdote or looked up the statistic I'd just mentioned. If what I'd first described as a long line drive to right ended up being a bit shallower and softer, there was no reason to correct the record. I could also elongate the present tense. For example, I could watch a critical play at second base secure in the knowledge that the runner racing home from third wouldn't cross home plate until I finished with the action elsewhere. This took some of the pressure off and made the broadcast considerably less choppy and confused.

My play by play was a little better than in the first few games, but still nothing to cheer about. I'd started the season recording every game on my tape recorder, but when I played them back at night, I spent too much time cringing to learn very much. As we headed out, I determined to stop taping and stop thinking and stop worrying so much and just do it.

4

ATLANTIC LEAGUE STANDINGS							
THROUGH GAMES OF MAY 18							
NORTH DIVISION	**W**	**L**	**PCT.**	**GB**	**STREAK**	**LAST 10**	
Nashua	11	9	.550	—	L 2	3–7	
Long Island	11	9	.550	—	W 4	7–3	
Newark	9	10	.474	1.5	W 1	6–4	
Bridgeport	9	11	.450	2.0	L 1	4–6	
SOUTH DIVISION							
Lehigh Valley	12	9	.571	—	L 4	5–5	
Aberdeen	10	8	.556	.5	W 1	6–4	
Atlantic City	8	10	.444	2.5	W 2	5–5	
Somerset	8	12	.400	3.5	L 1	4–6	

Zac Stark runs like a giraffe. His long, elegant stride produces a goofy, exaggerated head motion. His blond noggin is instantly identifiable as it wobbles above the pack of jogging pitchers, in an orbit all its own. Big Bird without the belly.

Tall is a very good thing to be if you're a pitcher—altitude gives you leverage, which translates into velocity. Zac stands six feet six inches and he is left-handed, which is good, too.

In his first five starts of the season, he mowed 'em down. Zac complemented his natural assets with intelligence and control and found himself among the league leaders, with four wins. He was also among the tops in earned run average and signing rumors. Big-league scouts came out to watch him pitch and asked themselves the question circulating through the press boxes of the Atlantic League.

Is this guy for real?

Like a lot of big kids, Zac was slow to develop. "My first couple of years in high school, I didn't consider myself even a college prospect and I never envisioned that I could get drafted by a major league team. They put me on the varsity, which should have told me something, but it was really tough. I didn't throw as hard as some of the kids when I was fifteen or sixteen even, but I got bigger and stronger and every year it seemed like I added three or four miles an hour on my fastball."

Drafted by the Florida Marlins, Zac spent two summers in rookie ball, which he described as the worst experience of his life. Rookie ball is the first and lowest rung of the minor league ladder. There are two of these leagues, one in Arizona, the other in Florida, based in the parent clubs' spring training facilities. After the regulars head north for the start of the season, their places are taken by a band of bewildered teenagers, kids just out of high school, for the most part. It's baseball's basic training. "You practice every morning and play games at noon, when it's 98 degrees and there's nobody in the stands. You're young and away from home for the first time, nobody has a car, so there's no freedom, and it's a very tough league."

Zac actually started his second season up in the Midwest League, but hurt his shoulder and found himself back in rookie ball. "After two years it gets old."

It's also a key moment in the numbers game, the ruthless process of attrition.

As Zac and the other players described the process, I couldn't help but think of a statistical graph that hangs in my office at home. It's an eloquent chart of Napoleon's invasion of Russia drawn by a French military engineer named Charles Joseph Minard. On the left, a fat red line represents the 422,000 men who marched across the Polish border in June 1812. The line is actually tan on the copy I have, but the French text says it's supposed to be red. The width of this colored band diminishes with every skirmish as the French army bled on its way east. In September, Napoleon took Moscow, all the way on the right side of the graph, the Double A level of this analogy. The line is less than a quarter of its original width.

Appropriately, Minard changes the color code for Napoleon's retreat to black. I imagine Moscow in flames as a hundred thousand survivors trudge back toward the left-hand side of the page. A chart along the bottom tracks the temperatures of that memorably nasty winter. At the Berezina River, it's 20 below. I don't know if that's Celsius or Fahrenheit, but at 20 below, it hardly matters. On the east bank of the Berezina, the black band is five millimeters wide: 50,000 men. The crossing was a disaster: on the opposite bank, the line is suddenly two millimeters thinner. By the time it reaches the Polish frontier on the left edge, the black line is but one millimeter wide. Ten thousand survived to illustrate why it can be such a poor idea to give one man total control of the team. Nap "The Emperor" Bonaparte was a masterful field tactician, but he clearly should have stuck to the summer game. A ballplayer's odds of making the majors are a little better than those of Napoléon's invaders, but not a lot.

Another way to think of it is to look at baseball as an enormous funnel that sucks in talent. At its base, the mouth is huge, big enough to include every kid who puts on a Little League uniform. At that level, everybody plays. Maybe one or two guys from each of those teams is good enough to make the varsity in high school, and maybe—maybe—one or two guys on that team is good enough to get drafted by a big-league organization. The next level, whether it's college or rookie ball, puts high school phenoms into games where, for the first time in their lives, they're playing against guys who are as good as or better than they are. The odds are that no more than a couple of the two dozen kids staring nervously at their spikes on the opening day of rookie ball will ever hear their names announced at a big-league ballpark.

For every kid who shows enough promise to be sent to rookie ball, somebody, somewhere, loses their job. Baseball, after all, has a fixed number of positions available. There are seven minor levels—Rookie, Advanced Rookie, Short Season A (most organizations skip either the Short Season A or the Advanced Rookie level), Low A, High A, Double A and Triple A—with 23 roster spots each. Add 25 more on the big club, throw in a few guys on the disabled list, and that totals about 175–200 players per organization. There are 30 major league teams.

Every year, each organization brings in at least 35 or 40 new players through the draft or various forms of free agency. When the new guys come in, 35 or 40 guys have got to go. A very few of those are major leaguers who decide to retire at the end of long, productive and fabulously rewarding careers, but the great majority are minor leaguers who are released. Cut.

Fired. It's easy to see how players can get paranoid: a lot of the time, it can seem as if their coaches and managers, the scouts and cross-checkers and player personnel directors, are looking for reasons to get rid of them.

One of the most important measuring sticks for pitchers is the radar gun. Even in a world of split-fingers, slurves and change-ups, the fastball is the best and most important pitch, and obviously, the faster it is, the better. An average major league fastball registers at about 88 miles per hour, so you'd think it would be fairly easy to dismiss everyone who doesn't throw at least that hard. Pitching, though, is more than velocity. Control and deception and movement are all critical, and none more so than that hard-to-define but easy-to-recognize quality called command.

As the owner of an average major league fastball, Zac Stark argues that scouts place way too much emphasis on the numbers that pop up on the gun. "Scouts use it to protect themselves," Zac says. "It's hard for a scout to go out on a limb for a kid who doesn't throw hard, but 90 miles an hour is its own justification." If the kid doesn't pan out, the scout can always point to that number to show his bosses that there was a good, objective reason to sign him in the first place.

Once in an organization, a pitcher is evaluated on his work habits, the quality of his breaking ball, his poise, and how well he does in games, but the gun is never put away. "One day I was in the locker room and was told that the minor league coordinator wanted to see me." John Boles, later the manager of the Marlins, told Zac that he didn't throw hard enough and cut him. "It was devastating. I'd only been in the game two years and I didn't understand how it works." He thought his results were pretty good, a 3–1 win-loss record and an outstanding earned run average of 1.73. Statistics can be deceptive, but it's easy to understand why Zac says, "I never saw it coming."

None of the other organizations saw a reason to sign him, so Zac found himself out of organized ball at the age of twenty-one. He'd been taking accelerated business courses in college during the off-season, but decided that he wasn't done with the game yet. In 1996 and 1997 he pitched in independent ball. "The first year it was the Big South, and then we went into the Heartland League. It was the same team but we changed leagues." His stats were nothing special, but he did enough to interest the Seattle Mariners, who signed him and sent him to play in A ball.

"I'm a borderline player as far as the major leagues are concerned. I'm not as talented as a lot of guys. That's humbling, and it can be very frustrating, too. There are games where everything is good, when I can throw all my pitches for strikes; and the next game, I throw like a rookie league pitcher again. Consistency is the difference. I'm not talking here about Pedro Martinez or Randy Johnson, there are very few who can dominate the way they do, but there are a lot of guys like me who can go out and perform at a very high level, but can't do it regularly. Sometimes that's talent or concentration, or, for a lot of guys, it's just staying healthy."

Or it can be a matter of keeping your priorities straight.

One of the guys with more talent was a right-hander named Matt Bacon, who started the 2000 season right behind Zac in the Arsenal's starting rotation. He and Zac played in the Mariners organization together and were teammates in Lancaster in the California League. Matt came out of a major college program as a third-round draft pick; Zac was taken in the thirty-third round out of high school. Consider those numbers for a minute: 30 teams went 30 rounds between Bacon and Stark. The experts might have overvalued Matt a bit and underestimated Zac, but one clearly showed more than the other. Zac agreed. "Oh, Matt had the skill and the ability, no question. Maybe he didn't have the stuff to be a number-one or number-two starter in the major leagues, but he was good enough to be a three or a four, absolutely."

What Bacon didn't have was the single-minded dedication that he needed to maximize his ability. "The situation with the Mariners was that he didn't accept baseball as his first priority," Zac said. "He loved baseball and competing, but he didn't keep baseball number one and the other thing second."

Allow me to be indelicate. The "other thing" was sex.

Matt Bacon was fervently, passionately and constantly interested in sex. While he was on the team, he sat across from me on the bus and allowed no female to walk, drive or bicycle past without a comment. One day at lunch at a TGI Friday's in Jersey with half a dozen other guys, he flirted heavily with a waitress who I would have said was not too pleased by the attention. When she was out of earshot, he trashed her as a "dog," but that didn't stop the steady stream of baldly suggestive lines when she returned. She didn't even smile at first, but he stayed with it and when we were done, she gave him her phone number along with the check. I didn't hang out with Matt much, but guys who did said this was typical. He had a large and, word had it, remarkably raunchy collection of pornography that he would offer to share as a way to introduce himself to his teammates.

I would also describe Matt Bacon as one of the brightest men on the team, and he could be very funny. During a rain delay one night in Somerset, he stuffed his uniform with towels, took off his cleats, walked out to home plate and did the old Rick Dempsey routine, a hilarious pantomime of a big slugger belting one and completing a splashy circuit around the tarp, finishing off with a headfirst slide through the puddles. Crudity aside, he was a good guy.

For a while, I thought his unending sex talk was a defense mechanism, a smart kid trying to fit in with the jocks by displaying what he thought of as jock behavior, but over time, it seemed to involve more than an effort to impress the guys. And, while Zac declined to provide details, there could be little doubt that Matt's obsession was the reason he was no longer on track to the majors.

"You can't go out every night," Zac said, "not all the time. You can do it and be okay for a while, but to be a success is so difficult, and the margin for most of us is so small that your priorities have to be different. Look at Darrell Green [the ageless cornerback of the Washington Redskins, then near the end of a Hall of Fame career]. He's done this his whole life, and that's the pattern to follow. You have to have discipline, you have to eat right and rest and focus to have success. Matt has talent, but there are very few people who can succeed at this game and *not* make it their first priority. There are a few of those, the real supertalents, but if you're not one of those, Darwinism will weed you out. There are so many prospects, such a huge player base, that there's always somebody coming up behind you. If you don't work hard, or if they don't think you do, if you cause problems on the team or, heaven help you, if you break the law, well, unless you're Michael Jordan, you're expendable. They know there's a kid in rookie ball who works hard and keeps his nose clean and throws just as good as you do."

Matt Bacon never got the wake-up call. He got cut by the Mariners and didn't change a thing after finding himself in independent baseball with Aberdeen. A couple of months into the season he and his roommate, a newly signed utility infielder, went on an all-night prowl in Bridgeport, overslept and didn't get to the ballpark until the fourth inning.

There are only two inviolable rules in baseball—be on time and play hard. Showing up halfway through the game is a capital crime. The infielder was gone before the day was out, and after a couple of days on suspension, Bacon was traded to another team in the Atlantic League, where arm problems and ineffectiveness soon relegated him to mop-up duties. Late in the season, when his club came into Thomas Run Park for a doubleheader, Matt announced that he hoped the first game would get over quickly: "I need to get to the bus and jerk off."

"When my time comes," Zac said, "I want to look back on baseball and be able to say that I did what my talent allowed. Maybe I'll go on from here to Double A or Triple A or even the major leagues, but if I don't get any further than where I am right here, there won't be any regrets. Maybe Matt will feel that way, too, I don't know, but I don't want to feel like what I did off the field cost me my opportunity.

"There are a lot of temptations. The life of a professional ballplayer is lonely. It's hard to come back to your hotel room alone every night. Even if you're married, you're away from your spouse and people look for ways to assuage that loneliness. There is drink and drugs and carousing and all of those diversions. It's tough to sit in a hotel room alone, and the schedule never lets up. We have, what? one or two days off every month? Every day it's the same routine: hotel, bus, ballpark, bus, hotel. There's an apt comparison to minimum-security prison, especially this year when we're on the road so much. This is what? our twenty-second day on this trip?

That's like living in a time warp. Your life is shaped by monotony, the rhythm of bed, TV, bus and out to the field. If you don't break up that pattern from time to time, you go insane. How many times can you watch the same *SportsCenter*?"

Even for a newcomer, the road routine got old very quickly. Early in the season, there was a period of early-morning disorientation that most experienced road warriors will be familiar with. I knew I could just grope for the phone book to remind myself what city we were in. As the road wound back through the same cities, I began to recognize the hotels by smell. The shabby Comfort Inn we used outside Atlantic City was the most distinctive for its odor of stale curry—the Bengali cleanup crew lived and cooked on the premises. Before long, though, I could distinguish the stuffy confines of the Bridgeport Holiday Inn from the crisper, better-ventilated air of the same chain's hotel in Nashua. Sound was a tip-off, too. In Newark, we stayed at a HoJo's out near the airport where the neighboring lots were stacked with wooden pallets and empty cargo containers that shimmied from the vibrations as the jumbo jets rumbled into the sky.

For most players, this dreary rhythm was forgotten as soon as the bus delivered us to the ballpark. There were routines there as well, but the late-afternoon sunshine, the supernatural green of the field and the challenges of the game to come triggered the welcome flow of adrenaline. This is what it was about; this was why we were there. Players talked of butterflies before their first at-bat. For me, that moment arrived ten minutes before game time, when the board operator back at the radio station played the taped introduction to the pregame show. I never opened my mouth to say "Good evening" without a tingle in the palms of my hands and a slight tightening of the throat.

It's different for starting pitchers, who have to await their turn in the rotation. When they're not pitching, starters are obliged to collect balls in batting practice. Most of them stand around in the outfield, shagging the fly balls that come their way and tossing them toward a tall screen set up behind second base. The guy who started yesterday's game picks them all up and, after peeking to check for line drives, ferries bucketfuls of new ammunition to the mound. Tomorrow's starter will chart the game, noting every pitch by type and location as well as ball or strike.

"It's a job," Zac says. "We think of baseball as a kid's game, and we all liked to play when we were young, but professionals have a chance to play as adults. Sure, sometimes it gets tedious to shag flies or do the bucket and live by someone else's schedule. You can wind up asking yourself what you're doing with your life and why you're here. But then your turn comes up, and you get to go out there and compete, and that's very, very hard and very, very interesting.

"On balance, I like the game with all its negatives. Being in independent ball isn't great, but this is indy ball done right. This is far superior to the Northern League, for sure. There are nice facilities, for the most part, better than Double A. Sure, there's still Triple A and the majors, they're better than this, but anybody who's played in the Big South League has no reason to complain. But I'm not here to kill time or play out the string. I think I have the stuff to pitch in the major leagues. If I can hone it just a bit, I think I can pitch on that level. I see guys on TV, they're better than I am right now, but I know I can get there. It takes a break, sometimes. You see guys in Double A or Triple A who have everything they need to compete at the major league level, but they never get a chance, or they can't take advantage of their break when it comes.

Baseball is worldwide now. It's incredibly competitive. There are only 750 jobs on the major league level and I know I may never get there, but I will never regret working my way up to being one of the two thousand best players in the world. If the balance shifts, I'll go play in a beer league and compete there, but right now I get to play against some of the best anywhere, and that's okay."

5

ATLANTIC LEAGUE STANDINGS						
THROUGH GAMES OF JUNE 2						
NORTH DIVISION	**W**	**L**	**PCT.**	**GB**	**STREAK**	**LAST 10**
Nashua	21	14	.600	—	W 2	6–4
Long Island	17	17	.500	3.5	L 1	5–5
Newark	16	17	.485	4.0	W 1	5–5
Bridgeport	16	19	.457	5.0	W 1	6–4
SOUTH DIVISION						
Lehigh Valley	16	16	.500	—	L 1	4–6
Atlantic City	16	16	.500	—	L 2	5–5
Somerset	15	16	.484	.5	W 2	7–3
Aberdeen	15	17	.469	1.0	L 4	3–7

*T*he road soon brought us to the Atlantic League's new ballparks, each nicer than the last. Despite the loneliness, in some ways traveling was easier for the ballplayers. Real ballparks have nets set up underneath the stands for extra hitting, better fields and mounds, plus proper clubhouses with showers and lockers and a fully equipped trainer's room. We looked in envy at the weight rooms and whirlpools available to the home team in some parks. In Aberdeen, there was still no word on a date for the groundbreaking ceremony for Ripken Stadium, which had been expected by June first. Anxious calls back home were met with assurances that the announcement would come any day now, but it already looked as if the Arsenal's new field might not be ready for the start of the 2001 season.

As Aberdeen looked ahead to its new park, it was interesting to look at how these other state-of-the-art stadiums—none less than three years old—addressed their opportunities and challenges. In Atlantic City, for example, the Sandcastle was situated to show off the skyline. The long neon row of casino hotels stretched across the outfield fence from the Trump Marina in foul territory way out past third base to the Hilton looming over right field. Because of the shape of the lot, left field was ridiculously short and the prevailing wind also whipped steadily out to left almost every night. The Surf led the league in homers every year.

To my eye, the Somerset Patriots have the most attractive of the new facilities. It's the standard amphitheater design, with a seating bowl stretching down both foul lines. From field level, ten rows of seats run back to a lower concourse, then ten more rows lead up to the main concourse, which is covered by a tier of luxury boxes above. The press box, concession stands and souvenir stores are all on the main concourse, protected from the elements. Most modern minor league parks are built like this, but Somerset's offered especially handsome proportions. The setting isn't much, though; railroad tracks run just beyond the outfield fence, but the trains themselves are invisible behind the billboards and you have to crane your neck to see Interstate 287 curving away to the west.

The Ducks' EAB Park on Long Island was very similar in design to Somerset's, and the grounds of an old insane asylum next door provided restful surroundings. Newark's Riverfront Stadium is the most distinctive architecturally. "The Den" was designed by HOK, the same company that sparked the revolution in big-league parks with Baltimore's beautiful Camden Yards. In Newark, they sensibly set the field to place the skyline of Manhattan over the outfield fence. It's even shorter in left than the Sandcastle, but without the wind, the distance isn't as big a factor. There is a rusted railroad bridge beyond the left-field wall and, in contrast to the shimmering, Oz-like vision of New York City in the distance, a foreground of warehouses and factories. The river the stadium fronts is the Passaic, not the Hudson. HOK used interesting brickwork for Riverfront and put the press box up on the luxury-box level, but there is no lower concourse in the stands and somehow, that long, uninterrupted block of seats just doesn't look right.

My favorite of the new parks is Bridgeport's Harbor Yard. The design is nice enough but nothing special. The setting is fabulous. To begin with, Harbor Yard boasts a transportation trifecta—busy I-95 thrums past the left-field line lit by the brake lights of the semis heading north. There's a ferry terminal just to the left of dead center field and the foghorns of the big boats bellow as they glide across Bridgeport Harbor on their way to and from Port Jefferson across Long Island Sound. In right, Amtrak's main line runs on electrified tracks elevated just high enough to make it seem as if their wheels roll on top of the outfield fence. Fans would shout "Hit the train!" as the 9:15 to New Haven clattered by. One night Mike Wolff just missed the northbound, launching a huge grand slam that bounced on the tracks as the passenger cars skittered away toward Boston.

Harbor Yard's tribute to twentieth-century industrialism is completed by the United Illuminating Company's mammoth power plant out past the right-field foul pole. This enormous Erector set blazes with lights, and beacons flash from the tops of the two tall, thin cooling towers. There was a lively debate on the team all year long as to whether those skinny chimneys would hit the field if they toppled in the right direction (no way). The entire complex always seemed surreal to me. I never saw a soul on the myriad catwalks and steel stairways. It looked like a movie set ready for the Terminator or the X-Men to blow it to fiery smithereens.

As interesting as that is, I fell in love with the oldest park in the league, the Nashua Pride's Holman Stadium, the "House of Thrills."

Holman is an ancient brick pile that offers plenty to complain about. The clubhouses are dark and dank and moldy, the dugouts are caves and the men's room urinal is a long, open trough. The press box is cramped and unheated and uncomfortable. Every night, public address announcer Ken Cail said, "Welcome to historic Holman Stadium." Up in the press box everybody snickered, "Prehistoric Holman Stadium."

But it's hard to imagine a nicer place to watch baseball. The brick-and-concrete grandstand was built in the old style, rising at a steep angle that provides unobstructed views for everybody. Even though there is an unusually large amount of foul territory, the clifflike construction brings the fans close to the field. For Holman's first sixty years, they had nothing but cold concrete risers on which to park their fannies, but the creation of the Atlantic League brought this stadium a new life. Blue plastic chairs were installed on top of the risers, a new section of bleachers and a picnic area were added down the left-field line and the field itself was resodded and leveled. They kept all the best parts, too: the fringe of tall pine trees, the smell of the fried dough wafting from the carnival-style concession stands and the nooks and crannies in the outfield. There is one spot in deep right center field where the fence zigs to create a very strange little triangle. An outfielder chasing a ball in there can't see home plate. I waited all season to see that. We played sixteen games at Holman, and not one ball went in there.

In the left-field corner, there's a low brick wall that celebrates the supporting role that this ballpark and the city of Nashua played in baseball's finest moment. There are three numbers in white circles on the fence to commemorate the players who broke the color line and integrated the minor leagues.

In 1946 Branch Rickey sent Jackie Robinson to play for the Brooklyn Dodgers' Triple A affiliate in Montreal and later that same season, he signed two more Negro League stars, Roy Campanella and Don Newcombe. Four of Brooklyn's minor league teams refused to accept the black players. Buzzy Bavasi, then the general manager in Nashua, said, "If they can hit the ball better than what we have, we don't care what color they are." So Campanella and Newcombe came to play in Holman Stadium.

Like most communities, Nashua's record on issues of racial tolerance is mixed, but this episode is surely worthy of commemoration. At the time, the players and their wives were the only black people in Nashua. Years afterward, Campanella wrote in his autobiography, "We go anywhere we want, do whatever we please and are treated like long-lost sons." That season, a local poultry farmer named Jack Fallgren offered an inducement of a hundred chicks for every home run hit by a

Nashua player. At the end of the year Campanella shipped 1,400 little peepers to his father, who used them to help start a chicken farm outside Philadelphia.

Those Nashua Dodgers are well remembered for another reason. With help from Campy and Newk, Nashua won the New England League championship that year. It will be a long time, if ever, before the Sandcastle or Harbor Yard can develop stories as interesting or traditions as strong.

On the other hand, if the Nashua Pride turn a profit, that will be a Holman first. The ballpark never worked out for its previous tenants. Most recently, the Nashua Angels-Pirates of the Double A Eastern League left after attendance tumbled from a seasonal total of about 138,000 in 1983 to 78,000 in 1986. Stung by the departure of team after team, most people greeted the arrival of the Pride and the Atlantic League with indifference. "Two years ago," general manager Billy Johnson told the *Nashua Telegraph*, "people looked at me as if I had four eyeballs and six noses. Now, I walk down Main Street and they want to know how the Pride did last night."

"A lot of people now find that this is the place to be," said Ken Cail. He's the team's media relations director as well as the PA announcer. Back when, his family owned the Manchester Yankees. "Already," he said, "this is the most successful professional sports franchise in the history of New Hampshire."

Cail himself can take a share of the credit. Entertainment is a big part of the minor league formula and Cail puts on the best show I've ever heard. This balding cherub takes electronic command of the ballpark from his perch in the center of the press box. A compact mixing console in front of him produces a never-ending sequence of sound effects, music and good cheer. Cail owns a rich, booming baritone warmed by self-parody. Between innings, he presides over the usual minor league hokum, and makes the dizzy bat race sound fresh every night.

There are more than a few fans who resent this entertainment. Some who've fled major league ballparks with headaches come to minor league stadiums in the hope that here, they will find a purer, quieter form of the game. This idealized image no longer exists, at least not at the professional level. Sound systems are even busier in the minors than in the big leagues. It goes back to the idea of family entertainment and the belief that kids will get bored and drive their parents crazy if there isn't something going on every minute.

They have two mascots at Holman: Shag, a lovable lion played by the wife of the scoreboard operator, and the hyperactive Monkey Boy. Shag cuddles small children and loses the base race to a six-year-old every night. The World Famous Monkey Boy sets off squeals of preteen excitement as he charges out of the Pride dugout to the thumping rhythm of "You've Got to Move It." He dances, taunts the opposing players, then grabs a Super Soaker and gets off a few shots before the well-watered kids in the first couple of rows bring their own squirt guns into play.

Nashua also did well on the celebrity-manager part of the marketing formula. Butch Hobson was a fine player for the Boston Red Sox, the third baseman for New England's doomed heroes of '78 who lost a 14-game lead to the Yankees. Hobson's later stint as manager of the Red Sox ended painfully after a drug arrest. After he worked through his cocaine addiction, he turned down an offer to manage a Red Sox farm team and get back on the big-league managerial track.

Butch Hobson is Nashua's third manager in as many years, but the first with such tremendous local name recognition and credibility. His pale face, blue eyes and white hair grace the team's schedule and media guide, he looks out on Nashua from a highway billboard: all proclaim BUTCH IS BACK!

"If using my name because I played for the Red Sox can help this franchise be successful, I don't have any problem with that at all." He also had a very good team, which didn't hurt. Tired of being also-rans, the Pride invested the money to ensure that their best players returned, and they recruited several more. The rule of thumb to gauge the quality of a team in the Atlantic League is to start with its number of former major leaguers. At the start of the season, Aberdeen had four; Nashua, nine. The Pride jumped out to the best record in the league.

A winning team, a famous manager, good fun and the classic ballpark attracted fans in record numbers, and Butch made sure they got their money's worth. On a Saturday night in front of the biggest crowd of the year, an Aberdeen player was called safe on a close play at second base. Hobson erupted from the dugout, went nose to nose with the umpire, threw his hat, kicked the dirt, waved his arms and jumped around until he was thrown out of the game. At that point, he ran over to second, plucked the base out of the ground and carried it back toward the dugout to thunderous approval. He grabbed a pen, signed the base and handed it to a kid.

Seasoned observers said they'd seen managers grab a base before, but as far as anybody could remember, making it an autographed souvenir was new. The Night Butch Stole Second entered Holman's legend, along with Campy, Newk and the chicks.

Sadly, Holman is an anachronism. The ownership put a million dollars into renovations, but the stadium has no economic future in the Atlantic League. Without luxury boxes, attendance almost doesn't matter; the team will do well just to break even. The Pride's lease on Holman runs through the 2001 season and if Nashua hopes to hold on to its team, the city will have to sink many millions into reconstruction or build a new ballpark. There are already rumors that the team will relocate to Worcester, Massachusetts, if Nashua can't furnish the kind of facility it needs.

Our first visit to Holman came in the second half of the long road trip, and Aberdeen was hanging in there. Led by Gil Martinez, the Arsenal offense lived up to the nickname. Coming into Nashua, Martinez was batting .413, T. R. Lewis .380, David Steed .359 and Victor Rosario .313. The pitching and defensive statistics weren't so great. The Arsenal had just dropped three out of four to the Ducks on Long Island and, after an all-night bus trip, pulled into Nashua's Holiday Inn treading water with a record of 15–16.

Friday night, Aberdeen took a lead into the late innings, but surrendered an unearned run in the eighth, then another in the ninth. The Pride won, 7–6. On Saturday night, the Pride was forced to use an emergency starter, a lefty named Dana Forsberg, who usually mopped up and also played the outfield. Forsberg pitched the game of his life. The Arsenal were shut out for the first time all year and lost 10–0.

Sunday evening's game was a humdinger. Nashua got a solo homer off Zac Stark in the first, but after that, the lefty shut them down. Johnny Isom drove home the tying run in the seventh and then the go-ahead run in the eighth. In the bottom of the eighth, the Pride got their leadoff batter to first base, but Stark reached back. He struck out the next two batters and retired the side on a harmless grounder. In the ninth, closer Jose Alberro redeemed himself for Friday's failure and blew the Pride away on a walk and three strikeouts. One out of three against the league leader wasn't too bad, and Aberdeen would get another shot against them the following weekend.

In retrospect, the week that followed was the crux of the first half of the season.

First, Yuri Sanchez was signed by the Cleveland Indians, who sent him to Double A Akron. No one could figure out why. Yuri is a smart, engaging, hawk-faced young man from the Dominican Republic, a switch-hitting shortstop who'd played his way out of the Mets organization. In two full seasons in Double A, he never hit anywhere near well enough to justify his often shaky glove. Now twenty-six, he moved over to play second with Aberdeen. His hitting improved, at least at first, but his fielding deteriorated. By this point in the season, he played only against left-handed pitching.

Cleveland needed a warm body. After a series of injuries, they wanted a guy in Double A who could back up at second or short, but why Yuri? Half a dozen middle infielders in the Atlantic League were playing better. Yuri's decision to accept the offer made even less sense. He saw it as vindication and deliverance, a way back onto the ladder that could lead to the majors. In the event, he would be no more than a spare part in Akron. A few weeks later when a prospect healed, Yuri was unceremoniously cut. Discouraged, he went back home and didn't play for the rest of the year. The best guess was that he was done.

The day after Yuri departed, T. R. Lewis announced his retirement. If Yuri Sanchez was by then a marginal player, Lewis was the heart and soul of the team, the number-three batter in the lineup and arguably the best hitter in the league. Even more important, he was the team leader, the guy manager Darrell Evans referred to as his clubhouse enforcer. If somebody dogged it, even a little bit, T. R. would let them know about it.

"I take a lot of pride in this game," Lewis explained. "I feel there's a certain level that the game should be played at. I always put the most I could into a game and I expected my teammates to do the same. If just a few of them don't give that level of effort every day, it makes everybody look bad, it makes the team suffer, so I do expect guys to go out there and give the game the effort and the energy it deserves. I feel very strongly that way and I guess maybe it did come out from time to time."

Theodore Roosevelt Lewis was drafted by the Orioles out of high school in Jacksonville, Florida, in 1989 and was on the fast track to Baltimore, an outfielder with four of the five tools that scouts talk about all the time. He could run, throw, play good defense and hit for average. Power, it was thought, would come as he matured. Just two years later, surgeons reconstructed the shoulder of his throwing arm. "They told me that, a lot of times, that's a career-ending injury, and in many respects, it was. At the time, you know, I was a prospect and it quickly took me out of that status, but I'm very proud of the way I worked hard and came back." T. R. batted well in three full seasons at Triple A, but never did develop a lot of power. Corner outfielders who can't throw well and can't hit home runs have a limited future. The Orioles let him go and he drifted from the Red Sox to the Braves and then to the Texas Rangers. By that time, his other shoulder was causing problems. "Finally, after a month on the disabled list in '98, the doctors said, 'If you want to continue playing at all, you have to have the surgery.'"

Lewis sat out the '99 season and focused on rehabilitation, but it turned out that there was little interest in a twenty-nine-year-old outfielder with long, lurid scars on both shoulders.

When he failed to catch on with an organization, Lewis signed to play with the Arsenal to see if he could open a few eyes. His bat was as lively as ever, but he needed to hit more long balls. "I'd spent a lot of time trying to get stronger, to see if my power numbers would go up, but I'm just a line-drive hitter, I guess, a gap-to-gap kinda guy. I'm not going to get under the ball a lot and lift it out of the park. That's just my swing and I have to get resigned to the fact."

Six weeks into the season, Lewis felt he no longer had a realistic chance. "I came here with a purpose, to get picked up by an organization. I won't say it wouldn't have happened, but . . ." His voice trailed off before he said that any team that was really interested would have called already, and that even if he made it back to Triple A, there was little to no chance to make the majors.

T. R. never said it aloud, but some of his teammates, maybe too many, did not measure up to his standards and play the game the right way.

"I don't get hung up on wins and losses and what other people deem success. To me, it's all about effort. If you go out and put the effort in, day in and day out, you earn the respect of your teammates and the other players. You don't have to have the big numbers to gain that respect, it's just the way you go about your business and play the game."

T. R. Lewis was a great hitter for Aberdeen, but as good as he was, the Arsenal would be able to replace his offense. They would never replace his leadership.

Aberdeen split a pair of games in Newark and headed back north for another weekend set in Nashua, holding on in the pennant race only because everyone else in the South Division was also playing poorly. On Friday night, Zac Stark was not as brilliant as he'd been the last time out, but pitched well enough and should have picked up another win. Sloppy infield play cost him the game.

As usual, Zac was the first player in the bus afterward, sitting alone in the dark with the little overhead light shining on his ever-present book. Victor Rosario, who'd committed a very big error in the game, made the effort to get to the bus early to talk with him. The conversation was already going on when I arrived.

"We have to concentrate," Rosario told Stark. "We can win with this team, but little mistakes have cost us. We just have to bear down, it's just the little things, and we are getting better. We've all been on teams with assholes." Zac looked up at the old shortstop. "This team, we all like each other pretty well, I think." Zac nodded as Victor continued. "We want to keep it together, but we can do it, you know? The pitchers are going good, now."

By itself, the pep talk was nothing unusual. The source was astonishing.

No one knew Victor Rosario's real age. Officially, he was thirty-three, but Dominican ballplayers have been known to shave a few years off their birth certificates. If rumor was to be believed, Victor may have lopped off quite a few. His face was deeply creased to accommodate a wide and ready grin. His favorite word was "dang," an exclamation that he varied in tone and expression to cover just about every circumstance. Once he dropped the twenty extra pounds he brought to spring training, he wore body shirts to show off his biceps. He had black curly hair he wore short and dark skin tingeing toward purple. Lady-killer.

Victor started playing professionally in 1984 and got his taste of the big leagues with the Atlanta Braves six years later.

The stat sheet shows four solid seasons as a Triple A shortstop, but he slowed and was back down in Single A when he was released from organized baseball in 1994.

After stints in the Western, Texas-Louisiana and North-eastern Leagues, all independents, the Atlantic League was a step up. Early in the season with Aberdeen he hit very well and established a club-record 14-game hitting streak, but drove his teammates and his manager crazy. Victor never seemed to hustle. He wouldn't run hard to first unless it might mean a base hit for him. In the field, he never tried to make a diving play to keep a ball in the infield. On easy grounders, he often held on to the ball, slapped it in and out of his glove then fired it over to first at the last second. This was just showing off. Worse, he held the pose too long at least twice that I remember and made the throw to first late. A couple of times, when Darrell put him at third base instead of shortstop, the glamour position, he discovered last-minute injuries and took himself out of the lineup.

In short, if there was one guy on the team who'd failed to earn the respect that T. R. Lewis was talking about, it was Victor Rosario. Now, after an egregious fielding mistake, he was taking the time to soothe the club's best pitcher. While few would pay a great deal of attention to what he said until he changed the way he played, this was an encouraging sign.

The next night, the Arsenal were down by a run when Rosario came up in the ninth inning with one out and Matt Taylor on first. Victor slashed a drive down the right-field line. Two critical things happened on the play. Coaching at third, manager Evans put up the "stop" sign as Taylor came around. In the event, the relay throw to home plate was well wide; Taylor would have scored the tying run easily. Behind the play, Rosario turned his ankle as he rounded first and hobbled into second. He was replaced by a pinch runner. Red-hot Gil Martinez was walked intentionally to load the bases and set up the possibility of a game-ending double play.

Danny Perez came up against Ken Ryan, a hard-throwing righty who'd pitched a couple of seasons in the Boston Red Sox bullpen. Overanxious, Danny chased the first pitch, a high fastball, and lofted a long, twisting foul down the right-field line. Nashua first baseman D. J. Boston raced over and caught it right against the fence, with his back to the infield. This time Evans didn't hesitate. Taylor took off from third as Boston whirled and made a blind throw to the plate. If the ball had arrived a fraction of a second later, if the catcher had to move his glove even six inches, Taylor scores. There was every chance that Boston would throw the ball wildly and let two runs in.

The throw was perfect, Taylor was out, and just like that, the game was over.

The loss hit hard. All season long, the team had suffered in the late innings. No one ever forgot the first two games of the year and they seemed to set a pattern. Now they were finding creative ways to lose. It was a new low point in the standings, too. The club had lost eight of its last ten to fall four games below .500 for the first time and the road trip still had another week to go.

In the Kilarney Pub at the Holiday Inn afterward, Darrell was furious. He was angry with himself for not sending Taylor home on Rosario's double and angry at Danny for chasing the pitch he popped up. "There are four guys on this team that are just fucking useless," he muttered. Dan DiPace wondered whether it might not be time for the coaches to control the players' bats more: put on the "take" sign to prevent hitters from chasing the first pitch, call for more bunts and hit-and-run plays to cut down on the big swings that produce pop-ups and strikeouts. Darrell, a big swinger when he played, hates the bunt. He almost always let his players swing away and try to drive the ball for a big hit.

As the next round of drinks arrived and he began to calm down, he spoke less of his and his players' failings, and more about the sheer brilliance of D. J. Boston's play. "How many times does he make that throw? Danny pops up that same ball, nine times out of ten we score. He makes the perfect throw, we get beat." He shrugged and vowed to continue to be aggressive as a third-base coach. "It's a percentage play. If you play it safe and then all of a sudden there's a bad throw, you feel, 'Oh man, I should have sent him.'"

In fact, Darrell was rarely aggressive and often held runners at third when it looked like there might be a play at the plate. Part of that was the makeup of the team. The Arsenal hit for a high average, so there was a decent chance the next hitter would do his job and bring the run home. Part of it was that most of the ballparks in the league had short fences; that next guy might well hit one over the wall, so why risk a play at the plate? Besides, more than a few of the players on the team were notoriously slow runners. More often than not, they were trailing in the game as well, in no position to risk making outs at home plate.

Perhaps it was coincidental, but it seemed to me that Darrell became more cautious after that play. Down the road, many of his players came to believe that he was costing the team runs. By itself this was no big deal, but it gave the complainers one more thing to crab about.

Danny, always the professional, showed no emotion on the field after he popped up. He was quiet on the bus, too, but so was everybody else. He told me later that he went back to his hotel room that night and had a good cry and talked to his dad on the phone. "My dad said, 'It's okay, just stop trying to do too much,' and he's right. I've been putting too much pressure on myself, trying to go 8 for 5, trying to get a double and a single on the same pitch. From now on, I'm just going to have fun."

It was also Victor Rosario's last game as the regular shortstop for Aberdeen. His ankle injury would be a long time healing. "It scared me," he said in his strong Dominican accent. "I've been playing sixteen years, and I've never been hurt like that, not my ankle, not my knee, not my arm, nothing. I didn't think there was going to be so much pain, you know, and it just hit me hard, it hit me real hard, especially at my age." As Victor continued to nurse the ankle, though, his manager and his teammates came to the conclusion that he was dogging it. When he finally pronounced himself ready, the Arsenal put him in the lineup for a couple of games to show that he was healthy, and then traded him to the Bridgeport Bluefish.

Late in the season, the Arsenal played the Bluefish in Harbor Yard, and Victor came out to play third base, right in front of Darrell in the third-base coach's box. He made two fine diving stops in the first inning and beamed with triumph. Take that, Mister Manager. After that game he came into the Carousel Bar in the Bridgeport Holiday Inn to rub it in a little more. Darrell wasn't there, so Dan DiPace and I listened as Victor talked about what he regarded as Darrell's disrespect.

"You know why I don't play third for him? He don't ask me. A man needs to be asked. Here, I play second, third, short, whatever they want, because they ask. That's right. Tonight, they ask me where I want to play, and I say third, just to show him."

Victor Rosario took pride in being a shortstop. His uniform

number was 6, the scorekeeper's code for the position. Third base was a demotion for him, an insult. It's possible he might have responded well to a sensitive request, but that wasn't Darrell's style. And Victor was completely wrong about that anyway. The manager never has to ask—it's his right to put his players anywhere he wants.

On the last weekend of the season, Bridgeport came into Thomas Run needing one more win to get into the playoffs. The decisive run in that decisive game was Victor Rosario's solo homer. As the Bluefish celebrated, Bridgeport general manager Charlie Dowd told him, "I knew I got you for a reason. One big hit." There was an edge to Dowd's remark. Victor batted very poorly after the trade, and while he might have hustled more, he still had very little defensive range. It looked as if Bridgeport might be the end of the road.

The day after the D. J. Boston play, the Arsenal arrived at Holman for a day game to find the old ballpark filled with kids in uniform. A baseball-skills competition was under way. The fastest runners, strongest throwers and surest fielders would go on to compete in a New England regional at Fenway Park, and the winners there would move to a national stage as part of the All-Star festivities in Atlanta.

Once their age group finished, the kids all stuck around to watch their older brothers and sisters and await the announcement of the winners. They mobbed the stairway that led to the visitors' locker room, waving pieces of paper, their gloves and caps and their uniform shirts, anything with space for a player's autograph. Not even a middle-aged stranger escaped: "Hey, mister, are you anybody?" Every once in a while, a kid would keep the pen out even after learning that I was just the radio guy. "We're all Pride fans here, wicked big Pride fans," a

T-shirted ten-year-old told me. He referred to the small pack of kids with him. All the others were just visiting as far as he was concerned, and he sneered at the outsiders. "We're here most every day. It's way cool."

I extracted relief pitcher Julien Tucker from the crowd and led him down into the dugout to record the pregame interview. "Were you ever one of those kids?"

"Oh, yeah," Tucker said. "I grew up in Montreal and used to hang around the players' entrance for autographs. I was a huge Expos fan." I tried to do the math in my head to figure out who his favorite player might have been. He was much too young for Rusty Staub. Tim Raines? Gary Carter? His answer surprised me.

"Darryl Strawberry. I always rooted for the Expos, but I remember one year, my dad told me there was no way they could win, because the Mets had this kid Darryl Strawberry who could win games all by himself." Tucker was a tall, skinny kid. "A lot of my friends told me I looked like him, so he was my favorite."

"Did you ever get his autograph?"

"No, I never did. I waited and waited, somehow I always missed him. But I did pitch against him one time. This was years later, obviously; he was down in Florida on a rehab assignment." During the season, injured big-leaguers are sometimes sent to the minors for a few games to play their way back into shape.

"So, what was that like?"

"It was amazing," Tucker said. He leaned back and smiled. "I don't think I was ever that nervous facing a guy before. He was my hero. And after that game, I got him to sign a baseball. I still have it, you know."

It was a warm, sun-drenched afternoon on a beautiful green

field. I let Julien go to accept the adoration of the pint-sized throng. Ushers arrived to shoo the kids outside as the grounds crew wheeled the batting cage through a gate in the outfield fence. There was no place on earth that I'd rather be.

Then I realized that I'd missed an obvious question. I found Tucker in the clubhouse.

"When you pitched to Strawberry that time, how'd you do?"

"Popped him up." The grin split his long face. "Fastball away."

6

ATLANTIC LEAGUE STANDINGS						
THROUGH GAMES OF JUNE 11						
NORTH DIVISION	W	L	PCT.	GB	STREAK	LAST 10
Nashua	27	16	.628	—	W 5	8–2
Long Island	22	20	.524	4.5	L 1	6–4
Newark	21	20	.512	5.0	W 1	6–4
Bridgeport	19	24	.442	8.0	W 1	4–6
SOUTH DIVISION						
Somerset	24	16	.600	—	W 11	10–0
Aberdeen	17	22	.436	6.5	L 4	2–8
Lehigh Valley	18	24	.429	7.0	L 1	2–8
Atlantic City	17	23	.425	7.0	L 5	1–9

*M*y admittedly limited experience in baseball leads me to believe that there is not a lot of crossover with the public radio audience. In four years, I met exactly one person who recognized my name, and that was another radio guy. Over the 2000 season, I did a series of commentaries about life in the independent leagues for NPR's *Morning Edition*, which has something like ten million listeners a week. As a result, a few fans came up to the radio booth to say hi and introduce themselves, but none of the players or coaches ever mentioned any of my stories. Actually, Zac Stark did say that his sister had heard one of my pieces—one that happened to include a brief interview with Zac—but he'd slept late that morning and missed it. This was fine by me. Given our schedule, I did my best to sleep through *Morning Edition* myself, and anonymity was part of the attraction. I would succeed or fail in baseball on merit, like everybody else.

In mid-June the *Baltimore Sun* did a feature story about me. The piece was nicely written and very complimentary, and the guys in the front office were thrilled to see a piece about the team in the big-city paper. I had mixed feelings. I worried that the publicity would change things on the bus. This was a baseball team, after all, and it wasn't right for the radio guy to get the ink. To punctuate the contrast between my old job and my new one, the *Sun* story emphasized recent political coverage, and I wanted to talk baseball, not politics. Earlier in the season I'd done some quick research on the presidential election in the Dominican Republic because Yuri Sanchez was interested, but I didn't want to spend any part of this summer on Bush and Gore or the impeachment or Hillary's chances in New York.

A couple of the guys kidded me for a day or two, but I don't think more than a handful bothered to read the piece, and none of them wanted to talk politics. Well, Danny Perez did, but that was just Danny announcing another opinion, it had nothing to do with me. The effect of the publicity was instructive, too. The story appeared on the front page of the *Sun* on a Friday along with a picture; my records report the attendance for that weekend's games at Thomas Run Park as 393, 781 and 410.

Darrell, though, picked up on a parenthetical mention of my experiences covering the Gulf War in 1991. "Is this right," he asked, "that you were held hostage in Iraq?" I said that it was. "I've got to hear about that." A few days later he asked about it again, when we stopped for lunch at an all-you-can-eat Chinese buffet outside Atlantic City. This is an incident that's enshrined in my bio on the NPR Web site, which is where the *Sun* reporter found it. I will usually tell the story when asked, but, while it's an interesting story, I like to think that it was one incident in a career. That day, I wondered if it was equivalent to the fact that when he was a player, Darrell was on first base when Hank Aaron hit number 715, the home run that broke Babe Ruth's lifetime record. Darrell says it was a great thrill, something he will always remember and be remembered for, but it's not like it was his accomplishment. He was just kind of there.

Getting captured is no great journalistic achievement. To the contrary. Once it started, I was a little like Darrell on first base, just along for the ride. There was drama and danger, but many other reporters have experienced much worse. In the same war, for example, Bob Simon and a CBS-TV crew were held for forty days in a notorious Baghdad prison. Terry Anderson of the AP spent seven years handcuffed to a radiator in Beirut. And too many journalists never came home at all. My colleagues and I were held for less than a week.

Also, reporters almost always fare much better than military prisoners. After I was captured, I kept thinking about one of the Coalition pilots who'd been shot down early in the war, who was shown on Iraqi TV reading a trumped-up "confession." His face was puffy and scarred and you could see pain in his eyes. I watched the tape with my friend Deborah Amos, who'd covered the Middle East for years. "My God," she said, "he looks like they've buggered him a thousand times. And they're perfectly capable of it."

There was no heroism, no defining moment, no catharsis; I survived. But if it wasn't the road to Damascus, there was a turning point on the road to Basra in the spring of 1991 that helps to explain what I was doing on I-95 nine years later.

I have a theory that "B" cities suffered disproportionally in twentieth-century warfare: Berlin, Beirut, Belgrade, Belfast, Bucharest, Baghdad, Budapest. With one glimpse, I could add Basra near the top of the rubble league. It's Iraq's second-largest city and its biggest port, and from a low hill just to the south, I could see the giant cranes on the docks along the Shatt al-Arab, the estuary formed by the confluence of the rivers Tigris and Euphrates. During the eight years of the Iran-Iraq War, Iranian artillery blasted away from the opposite bank of the Shatt almost every day. In Desert Storm, the Iraqi army's supply lines to Kuwait ran through Basra, so Coalition pilots devoted special attention to its railroads and highways and warehouses. Three days after the cease-fire, I could see a fresh layer of destruction, buildings on fire, entire blocks of smoldering wreckage. I got glimpses of the city only because every time I picked my head up to look out the window, I saw tracer rounds that seemed to be reaching for my head.

My view was from the backseat of an Iraqi Army jeep. That morning I'd hitched a ride with my friend Chris Hedges, a correspondent for *The New York Times;* and we drove from Kuwait City to check out reports that a rebellion was under way in Basra, that the Shi'ias of southern Iraq were rising to rid themselves of Saddam Hussein. As we headed north, we ran into several stragglers from the Iraqi debacle in Kuwait, some armed, most not. A few miles after the last U.S. Army checkpoint—a tank driver from the Vermont National Guard was kind enough to give us a couple of MREs, the nasty but nutritious plastic-wrapped field rations—we met an Iraqi soldier who told us it was all over in Basra and that the army was in complete command. As we drove ahead, I told Chris there was no way he could know that. "If he's right, though," Chris said, "we might find ourselves getting arrested."

Maybe ten seconds later, a jeep with three soldiers in it raced up from behind. Chris said it was crazy to try to outrun guys with guns, and pulled over. Two soldiers ran up, one on either side of our Land Rover, shoved AK-47s in our faces and jacked us down out of the car. There were no questions, no conversation, we were patted down for weapons and thrown into the back of the jeep. I was too stunned to be scared at that point, but Chris, who'd dodged death squads in Central America, told me later that he thought we had thirty seconds to live. "They always want to know something, why you're there, who you're trying to see. When they didn't say anything, I figured they were just going to shoot us."

Instead, our captors drove the jeep and the Land Rover into an army camp a couple of minutes ahead on the road. Chris and I were locked into a mud-and-wattle command hut with a cot and a desk inside.

"Let me do the talking," Chris said. I was grateful. He speaks passable Arabic, which I do not, and besides, now that I'd had a couple of minutes, I was too scared to breathe. After a little while, we were taken outside as a Mercedes-Benz pulled up in a cloud of dust. The back door opened, and an immaculately attired Iraqi colonel stepped out in polished brown boots, his field jacket draped around his shoulders. His black hair and mustache were cut in precisely the style of Saddam Hussein. He gestured imperiously, and soldiers quickly brought up an armchair, and, after the colonel was seated, they dragged up a battered old couch and instructed us to sit.

I tried to look brave or confident as Chris explained in Arabic who we were and what we were doing, but I was numb with fear. My brain simply would not function. I remember images—the contrast between the bare feet and ragged uniforms of the soldiers and their impeccably groomed commander. I remember gibbering something aloud, until Chris gave me an elbow. I remember especially how the colonel casually stroked the Beretta holstered on his belt as he listened.

A few minutes later another Mercedes pulled up, this one badly beat-up with the windows on the left side broken out. Four men in civilian clothes emerged. One of them, the tall one, told us they were reporters, two from Brazil, a Uruguayan and a Catalan, and that they'd been held there for two days, and then we all realized that the colonel had made a decision. Men with guns pushed us toward the old Mercedes and the jeep that had captured us. As we went, I could see soldiers stripping Chris's Land Rover. I wound up in the backseat of the jeep with Chris and one of the Brazilians. The Mercedes followed with the other three reporters and we turned back onto the highway.

As we drove north, we ran into a series of Iraqi army checkpoints. Each time, agitated soldiers fired a quick burst from their assault rifles to get us to stop and let us pass only after heated arguments. Chris couldn't catch everything, but said the soldiers on the road were saying we couldn't go ahead and our driver replied that he had his orders. We topped a slight rise, and saw Basra below.

As we raced through the city, I saw the green flag of the insurgents flying from the upper stories of a concrete building. I could hear the flat crack of cannon fire and the poppity-pop of small arms. Logic told me that the thin metal of the car door afforded no protection whatsoever, but as much as I wanted to keep looking, the impulse to duck was overwhelming.

We got through it and drove on to the campus of Basra University—like most of the signs we saw in Iraq, it was spelled out in both Arabic script and English letters—and parked outside the administration building. An officer came up. "Welcome," he said. "Welcome. You are our guests." The officer did not identify himself or his unit, but it looked very much as though we'd been delivered to the headquarters of a Republican Guard division. After a few minutes, different drivers arrived, who drove us slowly past a long line of artillery dug in on the side of the road until we reached the science building. The door was locked, so the soldiers kicked it in. We were escorted to a small, sunny reception area next to a big plate-glass window.

It was the first opportunity we had to introduce ourselves. William Waak, a reporter for *O Estado de Sao Paolo*, was clearly the leader of the group. He was tall and thin and, despite several days of grime, boredom and occasional terror, debonair. His athletically built photographer, Helios Campos, was younger and quieter. The energetic Antonio Castel worked for *El Observador* in Barcelona, and small, dark Carlos Pauletti for *El Pais* in Montevideo. I noticed that Carlos was working a piece of metal in his hand and, curious, I pointed at it. He held up a bit of silvery wire that he'd twisted to form the word "HELP" in letters three inches high. He shrugged eloquently. We laughed.

All of us spoke at least a smattering of English, but many

Iraqis did, too. In search of a more private common language, Christ first suggested Spanish, which Helios and I couldn't speak, and then French. Everybody agreed, though I had some reservations. I understand French vocabulary fairly well, but verb tenses are beyond me. Captivity, it turns out, is very largely a present-tense experience, so this didn't matter much.

Our new friends told us that they'd been taken on the road very much as we had. The first day they were allowed the run of the camp, then the Iraqis got nervous for some reason and locked them inside a hot, airless trailer. William said they became frightened enough to plan an escape attempt, when our arrival changed things. Because there were suddenly six of us or because two were Americans, or maybe because one was from *The New York Times*, the colonel decided to pass us up the chain of command.

Some officers arrived and took us upstairs, one at a time, for questions. I think we all worried for our fingernails, but this may have been the gentlest interrogation in the history of the Iraqi army. William, the first to go upstairs, rejoined us after a few minutes and said they'd started with a joke: the birth date on your passport couldn't be right, he was told, he looked much younger. Chris, next in line, came back to say that his session started the same way and that they seemed to accept that we were journalists. Since they let those who'd already been questioned rejoin the rest of us, it looked as if this was just a formality.

Even so, I dreaded the walk upstairs when my turn came. They started me with the same routine. I knew it was coming, I knew it was supposed to be a joke, and still, I froze. Once I calmed down, they asked if I knew I had entered the country illegally. Well, yes. Why had I come? We were journalists, I said, trying to report on the situation in Basra. What about our car, they asked, was our car from the CIA? No, Avis. My mind finally started working well enough to realize that they had my passport. I'd left it in the pocket of my jacket back in the Land Rover, but somebody had obviously brought it along. I also noticed that one of the officers was taking notes, and that was good news, too. Thanks to the universal military compulsion for record keeping, there was now a document with names and dates and places on it. If we vanished, at least there would be a paper trail.

It was getting dark by the time they finished and our guards took us outside to a small gatehouse. To our right, the Iraqi artillery fired a shell off toward Basra from time to time. There was small-arms fire, too, but most of it sounded pretty far away. As night fell, the Iraqis lofted parachute flares to illuminate their perimeter, umbrellas of green-and-red light punctuated by the white dotted lines of tracer bullets. Our guards began to sing softly in Arabic, and Carlos, our Uruguayan, replied with a ballad in Spanish; a tango, he said. Then there was a sudden and alarming surge of gunfire, and the distinctive sound of mortars. Incoming.

Our guards hustled us back into the science building, to the reception area first, then, after we pointed anxiously at the enormous plate-glass window next to us, they moved us to an interior hallway. Later they locked us into the computer lab for the night.

After it became quieter, I beat myself up. I'd screwed up before in my life, but this, I told myself, was spectacularly stupid. I don't think any of us slept. I know I didn't. I thought it was the worst night of my life.

The gunfire ebbed away by morning. We were taken outside to pee, our first bathroom break since we'd been captured. There was a low, evil sky. The dark clouds were tinged by the dingy smoke of the oil fires still burning in Kuwait, and a cold rain fell in great, greasy, gray globs that stained everything they touched.

There was no breakfast, but there was news. We were going to drive to Baghdad. Chris, Helios and I crowded into the back of a jeep next to a tough-looking officer, Major Assam. Our driver, Corporal Abbas, turned and gave each of us a smile and the grim First Lieutenant Hamid rode shotgun. The other three reporters were given a new driver but the same old Mercedes, and we joined a convoy of about a hundred and fifty vehicles. Most were jeeps and trucks, but there were a few tanks and armored personnel carriers, towed artillery pieces, anti-aircraft cannon and some command vehicles.

After a few miles on a highway, we turned onto an unpaved track that had been churned to goop by the tanks. Behind us, I could see that the Mercedes slithered around quite a bit in the mud, but we slowly sloshed toward a pontoon bridge that stretched across a lake. We could see the remains of both the original concrete structure and an earlier pontoon bridge that had been blown up by Coalition aircraft. Unless my mental map was completely off, this had to be Fish Lake, a substantial body of water just north of Basra that saw some of the bloodiest battles of the Iran-Iraq War. The heaviest vehicles, the tanks and the APCs, drove slowly across the bridge one by one, and the rest of the column followed.

To get to Baghdad, we would have to cross the Euphrates River as well, and once we got back on the highway, big road signs announced that we were approaching al-Ournah, the modern town associated with the biblical city of Ur. We could see ziggurats and what looked like ancient kilns off the side of the road. Of course, the bridges across the Euphrates were down as well and we pulled off the highway again, this time into a Shi'ite village. People walking along the side of the road carried their shoes in their hands and tucked the hems of their long robes into their belts as they slogged through knee-deep mud. The ground was so fluid that it looked as if the roots of the great palm trees were all that kept the land from being washed away. When we got out for another pee break, Lieutenant Hamid nervously told us that if any of the locals asked, we should say we were Yugoslavs, not Americans.

After a while, we learned that between the rain and the spring flood, the river was flowing too high and too fast for the tanks to make it over the pontoon bridge ahead. There was some tidal effect even this far inland and we would wait for the ebb. Major Assam went scrounging and returned with a handful of dates, a can of peas and a bottle of water. We shared the food and passed around the bottle. The water was salty and clouded with sediment and we debated whether to drink it. Obviously, there was a good chance that it would make us sick, and in our circumstances, even the lightest dose of diarrhea would be very difficult. In the end, there was no choice. You can go for quite some time on little or no food—all of us were graduates of the Kuwait Watchers diet plan—but you cannot survive without water.

The convoy was jammed bumper to bumper on the narrow main street of the village. "I sure hope those peace talks are going well," I said and scanned the sky. The last thing I wanted to see was an A-10 Warthog lining up a juicy target. Chris pointed out that the Iraqis didn't seem concerned enough to send out any patrols, at least none that we could see, and most of the soldiers took the opportunity to catch some sleep as the day dragged on.

Late in the afternoon, word came to get moving. Corporal Abbas connected the wires torn out of the ignition to start the engine, and just as we lurched forward, gunfire erupted, much louder, much closer than the night before. AKs chuttered from up ahead, then from our left. I jumped out of the jeep and went facedown in the thin mud on top of the cobblestones. Abbas started to maneuver the car, and as I crawled out of his way, I looked up to see Major Assam standing over us. From the Mercedes, William led Carlos and Antonio down an alley off to the right and called to us to follow. Firing bursts from his Kalashnikov, Assam protected our rear as we ducked down the alley and around the corner of a building. He continued to stand in the line of fire to command the alley.

Time is notoriously elastic in such situations, but it seemed as if the gunfire eased up after about ten minutes. Major Assam led us back to the jeep. While we'd been away, the convoy had become hopelessly snarled. Some of the vehicles still pointed toward the pontoon bridge, but others had turned around, our jeep among them, and many more were betwixt and between. Drivers and officers shouted angrily as they tried to untangle the tanks, and then the rebels opened up again.

Major Assam told us to stay put, and we crunched down on the floor. He fired out the right front window, but I couldn't see what he was shooting at. When his bullets ran out, he quickly fitted a new banana clip, fired off a burst and handed the empty magazine to Helios. He hurriedly gestured to a pouch where he kept ammunition, and stopped shooting for a moment to show the puzzled photographer how to load in the bullets. Again, it seemed like a long time, but was probably only a couple of minutes until Assam indicated that we should get out of the car. Antonio, who was on top of me, sobbed as he crawled over me toward the door. "The other way!" I yelled. The rebels were shooting from that side of the car. "The other way!" I forgot to speak French, but I pushed and shoved and finally convinced him.

The jeep was on a concrete bridge over a small stream in

full spate. As we crouched batween the car and a low wall on
the side of the bridge, I realized that my brain was working.
Don't get me wrong, I was really, really scared, but the numb-
ing fog of the day before had lifted. I could function. The
sound was unforgettable, some bullets zipping by, others
buzzing like bumblebees. Looking up, it was chaos. Most of
the Iraqi soldiers were hosing the sky with long, useless bursts
of gunfire. Finally, the tanks worked their way free and their
cannon gouged great chunks out of the buildings up ahead and
across the street. Several times, we heard officers ask each
other, in Arabic, "Army?" The Republican Guards thought
they might be under attack by a unit of their own army.

We got back in the jeep. Lieutenant Hamid was nowhere to
be seen, so I took the front seat, which left room enough for
Chris and Helios and Assam in the back. Chris turned to the
major to thank him. He meant to call him "brother" but by
mistake, used the word for "son." Clearly moved, Assam took
off his black beret and embraced Chris. For the first time, we
could see that he was bald on top. Then he made sure we all
knew how to load AK-47 ammunition magazines.

It was almost completely dark by this time. There was still
some gunfire, but less and more distant. The Iraqi command
car was just in front of us and while we couldn't overhear the
debate that was under way, we could understand the dilemma.
They could advance or retreat, but either way, the convoy
would have to unscramble itself first, which would mean turning on the headlights. Even on a rainy night, the glow would
be visible for many miles, an invitation for another ambush.
They decided to do neither and stay put, where the rebels
didn't need lights to know where we were.

Major Assam went off to help patrol the village and we settled in for a very long night. We were all soaked from the mud

and rain and a chilly day turned cold. Corporal Abbas started the motor a couple of times to get the heater going. My teeth chattered loudly and in the middle of the night, he gave me his sweater. The tanks fired their main guns every half hour or so, just to show that they were awake and dangerous. The Mercedes was parked next to a T-72 and the springs on the old car rocked for five minutes every time it let loose. We were right next to a gasoline truck, and I couldn't help but imagine a twelve-year-old rolling a hand grenade underneath it.

By morning, the rain had cleared. We had no way to know, but the worst was over. After the convoy sorted itself out, most of the vehicles went ahead over the Euphrates. We didn't go along. A small escort took us to an army camp on the south side of the river where we had to say good-bye to Assam and Abbas. When they asked if they could stay with us, they were told to return to their unit. We'd known these men for only a day, but all of us felt a strong bond. I was desolated as I watched them leave and even Chris, who'd been so strong, sagged visibly.

The Brazilians, though, didn't miss a beat. Within a few minutes, William and Helios started kicking a box of matches back and forth and soon got our new guard involved. He then taught us an Iraqi children's game called *baat*, which involved putting your hands underneath a blanket and guessing which fist held the prize. A few minutes later, a hatchet-faced Iraqi captain walked in and went white when he saw his soldier playing patty-cake with his AK-47 propped against the wall, but the ice was broken.

The next day, helicopters arrived to take us to Baghdad. As we'd feared all along, the army turned us over to the secret police, but, like our military interrogators, they had clearly been instructed to be nice. We met up with a much larger group of reporters, most of them French, who'd been picked up trying to cover the cease-fire negotiations. There were a few Americans among them, including a CNN crew and two GIs, First Lieutenant Kevin Rice and PFC Lynn Jeffries. Lieutenant Rice had borrowed a Humvee from his motor pool sergeant to go to visit his brother in another outfit and got lost. As we totted up all the stuff the Iraqis had taken, my contribution was modest, an NPR reporter's kit with a brand-new tape recorder. Chris assured me there would be no problem with the *Times* writing off the Land Rover. I've always wondered what happened the next time Lieutenant Rice went down to the motor pool to ask for a vehicle.

After a couple of days in a shabby Baghdad hotel, the Iraqis turned us over to the International Committee of the Red Cross and we left overland, on a bus to Amman, Jordan. Along the way, I'd finagled my passport back and puzzled the Jordanian immigration officials, who tried to figure out the bewildering confusion of entries without exits and exits without entries.

The Brazilian embassy in Amman threw a party for us the next day. We all did our level best to get drunk, but never managed to overcome the adrenaline still surging through our systems. Now that it was over, we could finally tell each other how scary it was and how incredibly lucky we'd been. We got through it with no injuries and nobody got sick. I called home, filed my stories and told everybody that I was fine. After a couple of weeks off, I went back to work and late that spring I was back in Iraq, the northern part this time, to report on the tragic end to the postwar rebellion against Saddam in Kurdistan.

That was my last war. I sat out the fighting in Bosnia and covered the conflict in Kosovo from the safety of the Pentagon basement. I had a lot of explanations for this. My wife and kids were one excuse—surely I'd put them through enough already. When my bosses at work asked me what I wanted to do now, I blinked. When given specific assignments, I did fine, but came up with very little on my own.

I have always struggled with a tendency for passivity, and it took me a long time to realize that this was different. I had scared myself silly. I don't know enough about psychology to weigh fear against humiliation and loss of control, but the result was a mild form of paralysis. I also knew that many others had suffered far more than I had and didn't think that my minor escapade justified counseling or therapy, but I now believe that was wrong. I nursed irrational shame and guilt.

By any objective standard, the trip was a success. I had a dramatic firsthand account of a bold Shi'ia rebellion, we'd seen Iraqi efforts to suppress it and, from watching villagers and soldiers collect their drinking water from shell holes and puddles, we knew that disease and malnourishment would be the next story. Still, I felt I had failed. In the course of my job, I've interviewed several former POWs, men who survived the Bataan Death March or the Hanoi Hilton, and was surprised to find that this sense of failure was not unusual, and maybe common. It doesn't make a lot of sense, but there it is. Men whom others, including me, regard as heroes told me they don't think they did anything special. They survived. Part of the ordeal, it turns out, is the guilt of giving in to your fear.

The other side of the problem was the rush. There is, as Winston Churchill observed, very little more exhilarating than to be shot at and missed. By comparison, Washington politics, even Bill Clinton's impeachment, seemed dull. I recognized the symptoms of adrenaline addiction, the affliction that drives some reporters from one hot spot to the next. I'd felt so alive, everything was so vivid and my emotions scaled up in response.

I don't want to overstate the effect of this experience. I was not crippled. I continued to function at a high level. I was diminished; less ambitious, less focused, more isolated. Scared. Rereading a letter I wrote to my kids on Father's Day, I realized I'd been thinking about it a lot on the road with the Arsenal.

Well, this is a funny old Father's Day. With me in Aberdeen and Casey in Florida, Connor is the only one of us at home on a day that we have always spent together. I kept all of the crayoned cards you guys drew when you were little—I treasure them. Every time I come across them I smile. As you guys grow up and move on, I expect I may cry when I see them. Or do what Superman used to when overcome with emotion: (choke).

The gift that is most pertinent to this summer is the little clay devil that Connor made in school and gave me in 1991: I call it my writing devil. I took it with me to Kurdistan when I went back to Iraq. It's been over my desk at work for almost ten years, and it's on my bedside table here at the house in Aberdeen. One of the legs broke off years ago and was lost. The other one snapped off more recently— I still have it—but the legless figure is hard to prop up on its own, so I lean it up against a book or a tissue box. The Romans worshiped a class of household gods far below the level of Jupiter and Mars, a group of workaday spirits called lares and penates. I forget the distinction, but surely this little devil is one or the other. And I will need its inspiration if I'm to finish the book I've contracted to write about this strange summer.

I think it's to be a book about transitions. Some of the ballplayers I'm watching are coming of age, learning the extent of their abilities and mastering their skills. And learning how to accept responsibility and—much harder—defeat. Becoming men. Others are beginning to understand that they will not be able to play this game much longer; age is eroding their speed and strength. They are looking ahead to a new and frightening phase of their lives. Baseball, after all, is all, or at least most, of what they've known. Still others are in denial, taking the game as an excuse for an extended adolescence that, in some cases, they have carried into their thirties. Though they're at a level of the game when objective reality suggests that they might want to reevaluate their prospects, they continue to take ever-diminishing adoration as their due and justification. A few are dissipating their exceptional skills in dissolution—alcohol, lassitude and obsessive sex.

Of course, I'm in transition, too. Not necessarily into a new profession—I have no idea whether I will do this again or not. I will admit that, for the first few weeks of the season, I did worry seriously about getting canned. My broadcasts were hesitant, replete with mistakes and corrections, without rhythm and narrative and flow. Well, I've gotten better. I've been in radio long enough to know that things have smoothed out considerably. I may not be in Jon Miller's class—no one is—but I can do this. Sometimes, when I relax into it and let the game carry me along, I think I can do this as well or better than a lot of the guys in the majors. But even if I am good enough, there are only about sixty of these jobs on the planet. Those who have them guard them jealously; there are hundreds with more experience than I eager to take their places and getting so much as a courtesy interview for an opening is as likely as getting hit by lightning. I've been lucky so far, and I believe in myself—I've taken advantage of the opportunities luck has presented. But I don't know about the big time, and I'm not sure we can afford much more time in the minors.

One real bit of luck—and again, I understand that people make their own luck—is the chance to write this book. I've always been intimidated by books, but have always imagined myself as a writer. Well, I will never have a better shot. If I can't do it here and now, I never will. And if I turn out to be good at it, and if it's success (not the same thing at all), that might be a more important career move than the play by play. Again, I don't know, and there's no way to know.

But the true opportunity this season is the chance to use the surge of conflicting emotion that we refer to as midlife crisis to rethink what I've done and what I'm doing. People my age, guys I know, are beginning to die. Not from stuff like car accidents or suicide that can happen to people your age, but from heart attacks and cancer. I'm sure both of you have thought about ending it all on occasion—everybody does, and I sure did when I was a teenager—but the

Big Casino doesn't leave you any choice. I've been shot at and threatened and shelled and rocketed and bombed. Mortal disease is different. One might. The other most definitely will.

So, quite naturally, I've reconsidered. Things at NPR have gone better than I ever had any reason to expect, but not so much lately. I think that's been my fault. For a lot of reasons, I've been both scared and bored. Scared to try new things and bored with myself. I've been stuck in a rut of my own making. There was a bottom of sorts last summer. I was frustrated and fat and beginning to feel trapped. I think the break happened when my sister Lucy called to say that she was sick and that it might be a matter of a few months or so. Turned out she and her doctors were being alarmist, but we didn't know that then. This was the biggest shout from mortality since your Uncle Mike died and it made me realize that his death wasn't an aberration. I knew I was drinking too much and retreating into a self that didn't interest me a lot and that I was not likely to break a pattern that had every chance to become a spiral.

I started running again. My back didn't hurt anymore, and this time I became religious about my sit-ups and weights—very little weights at first—and my back still doesn't hurt. Instead of hoping for a change to come at work, I saw this opportunity outside, and took it. Connor, I know you saw parallels to *American Beauty*, and I guess at least some of them are there. Working out—though I'm a long way from being as buff as Kevin Spacey got—and dumping a lucrative—for public radio—job for the minor leagues, but I think I'm a bit more self-aware and I have managed to skip the obsessive-sex part. This is, though, a chance to change the way I think about myself. A friend asked me what I was doing in baseball. "It's a chance to recapture myself." Interesting turn of phrase, no?

But you should know that one thing I've never doubted was the greatest piece of luck that ever happened to me—your mother and you. I may not express this at times, but you guys are my rock and my strength. I couldn't do this at all without her support and love (not to mention her earning power), and I never have to worry about what I might have contributed to the world or to history—I just have to think of you. You were both great kids and are turning into very interesting adults. I'm very proud of you both.

I know I've imposed part of the cost of this adventure on Connor, in particular. A lot of parenting is just being there, and I'm not. You probably can't help feeling abandoned at times, but I hope you know that I love you and miss you. Casey, I know you're off on your own life adventure, but I miss you too. A lot.

I'm sorry to have to send this to you in a medium as ephemeral and impersonal as e-mail, but you know I do everything on deadline.

Connor—hang in there.

Casey—write your mother.

Love, Dad.

It seemed to me that Darrell didn't react very much when I finished my story in the Chinese buffet. We finished our tea, and when the players at the other tables were done, we paid the bill and trooped back on the bus amid the usual round of insults and jokes. A few days later, though, he brought up Northern Ireland—another hot spot I've covered—and we talked about that several times. Looking back, I think this was a turning point in our relationship. Before, I was a listener; we talked about baseball and the team and I was there to learn. There was more of an exchange afterward. We discovered a common interest in science fiction, for example, and started to be friends.

7

ATLANTIC LEAGUE STANDINGS						
THROUGH GAMES OF JUNE 25						
NORTH DIVISION	**W**	**L**	**PCT.**	**GB**	**STREAK**	**LAST 10**
Nashua	34	23	.596	—	L 1	5–5
Newark	28	27	.509	5.0	L 4	5–5
Long Island	28	28	.500	5.5	W 1	6–4
Bridgeport	28	29	.491	6.0	W 1	8–2
SOUTH DIVISION						
Somerset	31	23	.574	—	W 3	3–7
Aberdeen	25	28	.472	5.5	W 2	5–5
Atlantic City	25	30	.455	6.5	L 1	6–4
Lehigh Valley	22	33	.400	9.5	L 2	2–8

I found it hard to keep up my bike discipline on the road. Atlantic League hotels rated somewhat less than four stars, but even the Comfort Inn near AC had an exercise room and on Long Island, we stayed at a Hilton with a full-blown health club in the basement. The stationary bikes left me no worse off than when I'd started, but virtual hills are easier than the real ones I had to face once we got back home. Then my host mom, Georgette, told me there was a back way to the ballpark.

"Instead of turning left at the end of the driveway, turn right, go left at the fork, left again at the T, and you don't hit the highway until Churchville, up by the Arctic Circle," the local equivalent of the Dairy Queen.

"Is it shorter?"

"No, I don't think so. It might be a little longer. But"—and she paused to get my full attention—"you go around Carsin's Run. There's no hill."

This was not exactly accurate. As soon as I turned right at the end of the driveway there was a nasty little climb rising on three tiers, each more testing than the last, and even after shifting my bike all the way down to granny gear, I was wobbling along red-faced by the time I reached the crest.

The first five minutes was the worst of it, though. There were ups and downs along the new route but no Himalayas, and it completely lived up to Georgette's description of "much prettier." I monitored the crops along the way and can report that the corn was considerably taller than knee high by the Fourth of July. My own progress I measured on my stopwatch. With more rolling and fewer hills, my commuting time to the ballpark dwindled steadily. After I got a little more used to the trip, I set myself a goal: an hour there and back.

My favorite part of the new route took me past the Harford County Airport. Weekends, there was almost always a small plane or two practicing touch-and-gos and sometimes a glider whispered over my bike. Once, a World War Two–era U.S. Navy T-6 trainer was parked outside the main hangar. The pilot told me it was a restoration that belonged to a rich guy who liked to keep it flying and let him borrow it sometimes.

It fueled one of my favorite fantasies. On a flight between Tampa and New York, George Steinbrenner's private plane suffers mechanical problems. Forced to land, the pilot settles the Learjet onto the runway right here in Churchville. Killing time while repairs are under way, "The Boss" scans the radio dial until he hears the unmistakable sound of a ball game. He sits quietly for a few moments, listening as the rich tones of the play by play man bring the game to life—the jokes! the insight! the stories! "Sign that kid up!"

The gate at the entrance to Thomas Run Park was the official finish line of my measured marathon and after locking up my bike, I usually walked back up to the McDonald's on the highway to buy a fruit-and-yogurt parfait, an orange juice and a copy of the *Baltimore Sun*. I brought a change of clothes up in my backpack, but, for the first several weeks of the season, there was no place to take a shower.

In the early part of the year, Arsenal players changed into and out of their uniforms in a white tent behind the concession stand on the first-base side. There were no lockers, just some benches around the perimeter and pipe racks for hangers. It was the kind of tent a caterer might have used for a small outdoor wedding and clearly never intended to stand for more than a day or two. After the first rain, a muddy stain began a steady climb up the outside walls. Inside, the humidity seemed to accumulate, and a couple of big box fans just pushed the smell of hot, wet plastic around a little.

While we were on the long road trip, Harford Community College let out for the summer and we returned to find that we had acquired a clubhouse. About a quarter mile past the left-field fence, there was a field house with a tiled locker room, showers and bathrooms for the players, an office with separate facilities for the coaches and a storage room that Jay

Tharpe adapted into a trainer's room. It was still small-time, but better.

My routine called for at least two or three trips between the clubhouse and the press box before every game in search of lineups and pregame interviews, a walk that brought me past the bullpen mound down the left-field line. I have a chronically stiff right shoulder, nothing serious, but I need to stretch it out, especially when I know I'm going to have to spend several hours sitting in front of a microphone. One day, I rotated my arm as I went past the bullpen and Rick Wise called out, "Hey, keep it loose! We may need you out there."

"You forget," I came back at him, "I go nine every night."

The line got a laugh and the exchange became a running gag that helped me remember that, like the players, I was at the ballpark to perform.

Doing it, though, proved to be more difficult than I'd imagined. By my third year as an apprentice in Bowie, I had felt entirely comfortable handling the middle three innings on my own and guiltily hoped for laryngitis or the sudden death of a distant, slightly loved relative to call Dave Collins away for a day or two and give me a shot at a whole game. This season, with 140 opportunities, the patter came slowly and I struggled to find material to fill the enormous expanse of airtime. How many times can you get away with mentioning that David Steed was born in Georgia, lives now in Arkansas, but grew up in Mississippi and would like to move back there after his wife gives birth to their first child, who, by the way, is due around Halloween? Once a game? Once a week? Every once in a great while is probably the right answer, but David Steed comes up to bat four or five times every day.

There was no color man to turn to for a funny story or illuminating anecdote; I was on my own, and at first, going nine was a problem. I ran out of material and shortly thereafter, I ran out of gas.

Eventually, stamina arrived without conscious effort. During the first couple of weeks of the season, I rooted for pitchers' duels, which are much easier to broadcast. There weren't a lot of those in the Atlantic League, though, and very few at Thomas Run Park. Cluttering both the mind and the score book, 12–8 ball games can last forever. Where a tidy shutout can be over in two hours and fifteen minutes or so, the slugfests we staged could run almost twice as long.

The breakthrough for me came at Long Island in mid-May. Zac Stark left the game with a 4–2 lead after seven innings, but the Ducks rallied against the bullpen and tied it up in the eighth. With the game on the line, there was a succession of pitching changes and pinch hitters, managers and pitching coaches visited the mound frequently, and when men reached first base, pitchers threw over repeatedly to hold them close to the bag. Both teams squandered several chances to score. Inning after inning, the game slogged on, and I was right there. However subtly every pitch changed the situation, I had it. Omens from innings gone by leapt to mind as needed, I could recap slowly, relishing the details when I needed to stretch, I could sum it all up in a couple of seconds when the action called for it. I was in control. Finally, an exhausted Duck reliever hit two batters to start things off in the top of the fourteenth, walked another, and grooved a 1–0 pitch to Gil Martinez, who drilled it to the farthest reaches of right center field, a hit good for two bases, three runs and the ball game. It lasted 4 hours and 11 minutes, the longest game of the year, as it turned out. Even doubleheaders and blowouts were easier afterward.

Following the big road trip in mid-June, Keith Lupton was

in the press box when I arrived to get ready for the first game of the home stand. "I listened to a couple of the games while you were away," he said. "Pretty smooth."

I'm not a good enough actor to have hidden either the anxiety when he started that sentence or the relief when he finished. Thankfully, his assessment confirmed my own judgment. I still had a long way to go, but I was no longer embarrassing myself.

At home, in Thomas Run Park, my spot in the trailer we used as a press box was all the way to the right, the home-plate end. The scoreboard operator crowded my left elbow, the official scorer sat next to him and there was room for three more people in front of the chair of the public address announcer, "Captain" Jim McMahan, on the extreme left. On the air I wore earphones, of course, but they did little to mask the buzz of the banter and the regular slam of the cheesy aluminum door as people clumped in and out. All of these distractions bothered me and I contributed to the problem by picking fights with our official scorer.

In the minors, affiliated and independent, the league pays the official scorers, but they are selected by the home team. The fact that the scorer's pittance comes from the league office lets everyone pretend that his decisions are neutral. In fact, every scorer in the league was a "homer" to a greater or lesser degree, skewing the hit or error rulings to help hold down the ace pitcher's earned run average or boost the batting average of a player competing for the hitting title. Players constantly grumbled about decisions that didn't go their way. A scorer in Atlantic City took a single away from Victor Rosario in our fourth game of the year that he was still complaining about the day the season ended. Statistics are understandably important to players hoping to impress major league organizations, but scoring decisions never affect the outcome of a game. It doesn't really matter whether a runner scored from third on a passed ball or a wild pitch. As I said frequently on the radio, that's just bookkeeping.

For some reason I felt compelled to correct Joe Stetka, who scored most of the Arsenal's home games, when I thought he was wrong. I'd look to my left for his decision, and roll my eyes or shake my head.

I blush to report that I railed at some of the board operators at the radio station, too. At first, I didn't understand that, except for Gary Helton, the station manager, they were all volunteers. In many cases, my baseball broadcasts had displaced their own programs. None had ever run the board for a ball game before and Gary was as shocked as I was to learn that several knew nothing about the game of baseball, not even the number of outs in an inning.

Given the rudimentary nature of our technology, broadcasting a ball game involved a kind of telepathy between the play by play man and the board op back at the station. He or she can't hang on every word—they have plenty of other things to do while I'm talking—but they need to follow the rhythm of the game. At the end of each half inning, for example, the cue to go back to the studio was the score: "And so, after four full innings, it's Aberdeen 4, Bridgeport 1." That sounds simple, but there are lots of other times that I gave the score during the inning: "That's an RBI double by Johnny Isom, Fowler comes around to score and Aberdeen now leads it, 5 to 1." It's easy for an anxious volunteer to mistake that as the cue and trigger the sequence of public service announcements and promos that ran for ninety seconds between each half inning. Pitching changes could be tricky, too.

Everybody, including me, made a lot of rookie mistakes and

I got frustrated when some of the board ops didn't seem to get it. One kid told Gary that he didn't volunteer his time to get yelled at, and quit. With school out for the summer, it took weeks for Gary to find a replacement, which meant that he had to pick up that shift himself.

Including Aberdeen, only four of the eight teams in the league had full-time radio announcers. Nashua broadcast only its home games; Bridgeport and Long Island couldn't find a local station willing to carry more than a handful of games and Lehigh Valley didn't have a radio deal at all. The only place we could find to install visiting broadcasters was up on the press box roof. A couple of beach umbrellas were supposed to provide protection from the elements up there, but they didn't survive the first thunderstorm. The Somerset Patriots were the first team to come through with a broadcaster, and I will never forget the expression on Dave Schultz's face when I showed him the ladder upstairs. In a somewhat strangled voice, he pointed out that if a storm came through, he'd be sitting beside a big stack of electrical equipment on top of a metal box in the middle of a big field. Not to worry, I assured him. Surely the tall backstop would act as a lightning rod. Since the chain-link backstop was only a couple of feet from the edge of the trailer, this was small comfort and we agreed to bring him inside if the weather turned ugly.

Schultz is twenty years younger than I am and got into play by play along a more traditional route. "Growing up," he told me at lunch one day, "I thought I might be a lawyer like my dad, but I realized fairly early that I wasn't enough of a student to do that. But I still wanted to be like him in the sense of doing one thing for sixty years that I loved."

Dave studied radio and TV production at SUNY Oswego. The recession of the early nineties made it hard to find a job after he graduated, but he found freelance work as a broadcast technician. "I was in Skydome for the All-Star Game and spirited a copy of the *Baseball America* guide out of the Blue Jays' front office. I'd never seen one before and I didn't really know what it was, but it had the address of every team, so I wrote to them all looking for a job. The first team to write back was the Richmond Braves, and they advised me to go to the winter meetings."

Once the premier venue for player trades in the off-season, the winter meetings are more important these days as a job fair for nonuniformed personnel, everybody from salesmen to groundskeepers. And broadcasters. "I'd never done baseball," Schultz said, "but I wasn't trying to get a job with the Yankees. I honestly thought getting a job in the minors would be easy. That's not the case at all. But I got an interview with the Wichita Wranglers, and they asked me to write a proposal about marketing—how to increase attendance.

"So I wrote a proposal after I got home and sent it in, and I remember"—and here he took his wallet out of the back pocket of his Dockers and carefully extracted a frayed ticket stub from a Syracuse University basketball game at the Carrier Dome—"I was at this game when they called. My mom took the message, and I called back and they offered me a job as a marketing assistant. So I went out there and learned what minor league baseball is all about."

I asked the obvious question.

"Sales," he replied flatly. "Every day, it's sell, sell, sell. The front office is a world away from the dugout, and the game there is sales and nothing else. But I was lucky, I was a kid and they gave me a very small sales quota and I filled it pretty quickly and I spent a lot of time that summer with the radio guy in the booth. Sometimes, when it was slow, I'd join him on the air for a little while but the brass didn't like that, they wanted him to establish his identity as the voice of the team. The general manager said if I wanted to do a whole game, that would be okay, just not the middle three. I thought that was a little strange, but I didn't complain. We had a doubleheader coming up, so he took the first game and I did the second.

"Of course, his game was a 3–2 pitchers' duel, an hour and thirty-six minutes for the seven-inning game and mine was 9 to 8 with back-and-forth action and the lead changing hands. It lasted three hours and my score book was totally messed up and I got totally lost. But that's how I started."

After another marketing job with High Desert of the California League, Schultz landed his first full-time play by play job with the Corpus Christi Barracudas of the independent Texas-Louisiana League, "affectionately known to intimates as the 'latex' league." He moved on to Peoria, and from there to Florida and the Double A Jacksonville Suns.

"There are a lot of owners in that league [the Southern League] that would be shocked to learn that there is a better operation in an independent league than any of theirs, but Somerset makes more money than any of them. This is an unbelievable area," he said of central New Jersey's suburbs. "It's the haves and the have-mores, and it's cheaper to advertise in this market through minor league baseball than just about anything else."

They also treat their broadcasters better. From 1994–99 he earned between $17,900 and $18,600 per year, plus commissions on sales. Like players, broadcasters are paid only during the season, so almost all of them do something else for the team, usually sales or public relations, and Schultz's salary was typical. With Somerset, he said he makes $30,000 plus commission, and is not asked to sell during the season. "This," he said reverently, "is a great organization."

But not where he wants to be. "I hoped to be in the major leagues by the time I was thirty, or at least a lot closer than I am. Now, baseball is the only sport that gives you the opportunity to develop in an established minor league system. How do you get on TV, news or sports? Same thing. You go to a small town and learn.

"When I was in Peoria, I ran into a guy named Ken Wilson, who does play by play in the majors and also does hockey. Now, I always thought hockey would be the most difficult game to do play by play, it's so fast, everybody plays offense and defense, the lineups are constantly changing on the fly, and Wilson told me, 'Your job is much harder. First of all,' he says, 'you're your own technician. If something goes wrong when I'm on the air, I know it's someone else's fault. And you're your own producer.' And then he asked me, 'Who's your first baseman?' and I proceeded to tell him a few facts about the guy, and he says, 'How much information about that guy is there in your media guide? Two or three lines? I go to do a game in St. Louis, and there's five or six pages on Mark McGwire. Doing a major league baseball game is the easiest thing in the world. You? You're doing sales, you write the game notes, you do the play by play and the color and at the end of the game, you pack up the equipment.'

"Now I've had myself a little career, I've worked in Double A, but I've never had so much as a courtesy interview for a major league job. I'm working to improve my broadcast, but I have to think that my biggest problem now isn't what I know, but who. Look, Darren Sutton got a radio job with the Angels this year, I think he worked, what? one year in the minors?

Somehow I don't think that my audition tape and his were in the same pile. He got the opportunity because his father is in the Hall of Fame and pitched for the Angels."

Schultz leaned over the table and spoke with great intensity. "Look, I know I can't compete with former players, I understand that. They bring something that I don't have. I understand why Vin Scully still does the Dodgers games after all these years and why Harry Caray wanted to do it until he died. It's a great job. It's like a first-class tour of American cities, and it's New York and San Francisco and L.A. It's a little different to ride the bus to Bridgeport or AC. I just don't know what I have to do to get the big break.

"Every other part of the business, they promote from the minor leagues. Ballplayers, trainers, even groundskeepers. Triple A broadcasters can't get anybody to even listen to their tapes."

I named a few guys who did work their way up to the big leagues, but Schultz waved them away as exceptions to the rule. So, I asked, if he doesn't make it to the majors, what's Plan B?

"Plan B? There is no Plan B. The only thing I might do if I don't get to the major leagues is to be an agent for broadcasters, as long as that doesn't involve going to law school. Or better yet, an advocate, someone to try to get the major league teams to listen, to give guys like me a chance."

Dave Schultz also points out that play by play can be tough on your social life. "I had one serious girlfriend, she was in TV news and she left to go to another city. Then I started dating someone else, and she immediately questioned my schedule. Every summer my family gets together for a week at a lake near Syracuse, a big gathering. I'm never there. The worst, the one that really upset me, was my cousin. This was a girl I grew up with, we were very close, and she's getting married in Beverly Hills. I'm in Zebulon, North Carolina, and I'm with my partner, who could have done the game, and my GM wouldn't let me go. I should have danced with her at her wedding. It was a minor league game that nobody remembers, and I know it's my job, but my partner is there and he could have done one game by himself. It was the Fourth of July, a Jewish wedding in Beverly Hills. How could I miss that?"

"Do you want permission to have sex on the road?"

My wife popped this question on me about a week before opening day. It was a bolt from the blue, but anybody who's been married for twenty years knows there is only one answer to this bombshell, and only one way to deliver it.

Pause. Let surprise settle in. Do not reply immediately or she'll assume you're lying. Thoughtfully, now.

"No . . . no, I really can't . . . well, I guess I can imagine a situation where that might happen, but I can't imagine not regretting it."

A few moments later, I went on to note how all the hotties gravitate to the fifty-year-old radio guy every time a group of twenty-something professional athletes walks into a bar. In practice, experience suggests that my appeal in such circumstances is limited to babes playing video trivia games, and that even that powerful allure vanishes when the subject switches from Geography of the Ancient World to *90210*.

Since I was on the road even when the team was home, Liane and I arranged trysts for the rare occasions when my off days coincided with hers, and these conjugal visits took on some of the characteristics of sailors on liberty. We had one day together in New York—the team was in Newark, where I had a free hotel room, but Liane nixed the charms of the airport Howard Johnson and we took a room in Manhattan. Later, there were two (!) days off in Nashua, so she took a cheap flight to Manchester and we ran away to Cape Cod. And I got home a couple of times.

As thrilling as it was to date my wife again, the long stretches in between got lonely. Friends came out sometimes to visit, but I was busy before and during the game. By the time I was done, it was often after eleven and since they usually had to go to work the next day, few followed through on plans to go out for a drink or a meal. Much of the time, the hotel bar was closed by the time the team bus pulled up. Television became far too important a companion and the peculiarity of baseball's schedule funneled viewing time into strange segments of the broadcast day. Late night, I caught up on Audie Murphy's acting career; midday, I tried to time visits to the hotel Exercycle to coincide with *Law & Order* reruns and even reconsidered the merits of *Magnum, P.I.* Of course, The Weather Channel was popular, too.

But the tedium vanished on the bus ride to the ballpark. The players filed into the visitors' clubhouse and I went up to the radio booth. Soon, we all reconvened on an impossibly green field warmed by the afternoon sun. Once I got into rhythm, I could almost always hang out at the batting cage while the guys were hitting. This was the best time to find out if this guy's shoulder was feeling better or why that guy was experimenting with a new stance. Rick threw BP to the starters, then Darrell or, when his arm was up to it, Dan, would finish up. Last night's failures melted away in the promise of a new day. As dreary as the bus trips and the hotels could be, I was never bored at work.

Halfway through the season, I got an e-mail of encouragement from Ken Levine, a onetime scriptwriter for *M*A*S*H* and *Cheers* who gave it up for baseball play by play. Levine did three years in the minors and I'd heard him when he shared the Orioles booth for a year with the great Jon Miller. "Let me guess," he wrote. "A lot of your friends think you're crazy for doing this. They don't comprehend how great it is to wake up each morning and know that your only responsibility for the day is to go out to a ballpark and call a baseball game."

Levine was kind enough to reply when I wrote him back, and we exchanged notes on the trade. "Never miss an opportunity to go to the bathroom." Excellent advice. I complained of mutant-dwarf foul poles and he recalled the poor lighting in minor league outfields that led him to title his book *It's Gone . . . No, Wait a Minute.*

Tellingly, Levine ended his message by adding, "Oh . . . and I hope you have a winning ball club. That makes it sooo much easier."

The Arsenal was not a winning ball club. As well as the team hit, spotty pitching, poor defense and the difficulties of the long road trip added up. The club simply couldn't put together a winning streak, and as the road wore the guys down, the losses started to come in bunches. After a sluggish start of their own, the Somerset Patriots pulled away from the rest of the weak-sister South Division. On the last day of the first half, we were in Atlantic City for a doubleheader that would decide only whether the Arsenal or the Surf finished in second.

There was a great kerfuffle under way when we arrived at the Sandcastle. Chuck Betson, my counterpart with Atlantic City, got fired after a screaming argument with general manager Ken Shepard. The Betman was a salesman as well as a broadcaster, a stout, cheerful, hearty man in his forties. I've often thought of live radio as thinking with the last tenth of an inch of your tongue, and Chuck Betson seemed to live a lot of his life in that stream of consciousness. With his sales hat on, he booked an event that required the presence of Splash, the Surf mascot, but, hurrying to put on his headset, he neglected to tell anybody. By the time he remembered, it was almost the last minute. Irritated, Shep told him that since he'd booked Splash without booking somebody to be Splash, he'd have to don the mascot suit himself. Affronted by the indignity, Betson went bananas. The dialogue quickly descended to will not–will too and at twenty minutes to air, assistant GM Mario Perrucci was startled to learn that he was Atlantic City's new play by play man.

Mario had done color with Chuck sometimes, so the booth wasn't a complete mystery, but he was enormously relieved when umpire Bob Willman came up to help him out. Aberdeen and AC were the only teams scheduled to play that day and Willman's crew was off. He lived across the street from the Sandcastle and had played a role in the construction of the stadium and the development of the league. Adam Gladstone, the Arsenal's director of team operations, himself a former Atlantic League umpire, was also up in the press box that day and finally redeemed a long-standing promise to join me on the air. After Willman finished his stint with Mario in the booth next door, he came over, too. It was great fun to juggle two guests and the play by play.

Willman is an interesting character. A catcher in his playing days, he still looks the part. He's short, wide and strong, more of a wrestler's build, really. He shaves his head and leans forward when he walks. He's a loud Rush Limbaugh conservative if he thinks you're a liberal and a combative libertarian if he thinks you're on the right. It's safe to say that Bob Willman likes an argument.

Growing up in Jersey, he umpired his first game at the age of thirteen. "I liked it," he told me. "I enjoyed umpiring as much as I did playing." He went to an umpire school after college, got a job and, like a player, started moving slowly up the minor league ladder. "Eventually, I spent three years in the International League [Triple A] and I didn't like my prospects. There were no openings in the majors, or not many, and I decided that if I couldn't make the big leagues, I didn't want to go on. I was drinking too much at the time, and maybe that was part of it. I'll never know. They never gave me a reason, but I was a serious drinker in those days."

In 1981 Bob Willman was out of work with nothing on his résumé except eight years as a minor league umpire. At the time, casino gambling had just been legalized in Atlantic City, so he decided to change his life. He quit drinking and went to craps school and learned to deal baccarat and roulette as well. "But I wasn't happy. The casino game stinks. Unless you love it, it's the same as any business." He got back into sports as a football and soccer referee.

"One day, I was at a wedding and I had one of those chocolates with cherries and brandy inside. I didn't think a thing about it. A couple of days later, I was out with some football refs after a game and they ran out of O'Doul's. There was a pitcher of beer on the table, so I had one. No big deal. Then I had one or two at a bowling alley and the next thing I know, my kitchen is full of empty vodka bottles."

Bob Willman took his last drink on January 4, 1997. He's been a crew chief since the start of the Atlantic League and says that Alcoholics Anonymous has helped him on the field. "I try to apply some of the principles. I'm not there to call a game, but to call this play, this pitch. And I've learned that everybody blows calls, but, you know, there are more important things in life."

• • •

That night was one of those broadcasts where I could feel everything going well; Willman and Gladstone traded stories about the early days of the league, Danny Perez and Tyrone Horne belted home runs and the Arsenal swept the twin bill to edge past the Surf in the standings and finish the first half in second place, which was not quite meaningless for an expansion team.

Between games, we heard that Shepard and Betson had settled their differences and that The Betman would be back to broadcast the second half of the season. Bob Willman also paid me a compliment, telling Adam how nice it was to work with a real pro.

"You should have heard him when he started," Adam said, and even as he retold the story of the weak waffle and the breaking bitch, it seemed like ancient history. With three days off coming up for the All-Star break, Liane drove up to Aberdeen to meet the bus. We planned to spend the night at the team hotel and head home in the morning. She started pulling in WHFC a few miles north of Baltimore and got to hear the second game of the doubleheader, the first time she'd heard me all year. The team bus didn't get into Aberdeen until about two in the morning, but she woke up to tell me that I sounded great. I like to think I know the difference between collegial praise and wifely support. She said she could hear me having so much fun that she knew I'd want to do it again next year.

It was unusual to have guests on the air with me, but there were a few semiregulars. The best were the reporters who covered the league, Tom King of the *Nashua Telegraph*, Rich Elliot of the *Connecticut Post* and Geoff Mosher of the *Courier-News* in Bridgewater, New Jersey, the home of the Somerset Patriots. Once every series, they'd come on for a couple of innings. Less frequently, executives like Frank Boulton in

Long Island or Charlie Dowd, the GM in Bridgeport, would sit in, too.

Those three reporters plus the four regular radio broadcasters were masters of a spectacularly arcane field. There are baseball leagues even more obscure than ours, but not many. We few helped one another out with quotes and anecdotes and information—it's not like we were in competition—and developed a camaraderie that's probably familiar to high-energy-particle physicists or historians of seventeenth-century cartography.

At the start of every series, I'd exchange notes and stat sheets with my fellow broadcasters, and consult on the pronunciation of any new players and their nicknames. An interesting moniker is radio gold. Julien Tucker, for example, is a dead ringer for the actor Jeff Goldblum, so the players called him The Fly. Yuri Sanchez turned out to be named for the first man in space, Yuri Gagarin, and we'd had Theodore Roosevelt "T. R." Lewis. Erskine Kelley was a two-fer. His first name was from Carl Erskine, the old Brooklyn Dodger; his nickname, Sarge, from the military manner in which he wore his baseball cap, a tribute to his father, a former drill sergeant.

Relations were always good, too. Jose Cepeda, who replaced Victor Rosario as Aberdeen's shortstop, was the nephew of Hall of Famer Orlando Cepeda, who was, in turn, known as both The Baby Bull and as Cha-Cha. The Newark Bears were a relatively famous team. They featured major league brothers Ozzie Canseco (Jose) and Mike Berry (Sean), major league son Russ Chambliss (Chris) and Bobby Bonds, Jr., who qualified on both counts (Barry, and Bobby, Sr.). I learned the best handle in the league after Al Sontag of the Bridgeport Bluefish dominated the Arsenal one day and carried a no-hitter into the ninth inning. Danny Perez broke it up with a twenty-three-hopper up the middle. Later, on the bus, he explained why Sontag is so tough to hit. "You can't pick the ball up off him, he's all arms and legs," Danny said. "That's why we call him The Squid." I was a little upset to get this juicy piece of calamari after the game, but it's a long season and I knew we'd see The Squid again before too long.

Diminutives are the most common nicknames. It's easy to see how a childhood "Jimmy" or "Bobby" sticks on a young player, and once it's set, it's impossible to change. Before taping a pregame show, I asked Aberdeen's director of baseball operations a standard question: "How do you like to be identified?" But I didn't leave it there. "Do you prefer 'Billy'?"

William Ripken is universally known as Billy. I never heard him called anything else through the course of his playing career, that was the name in the newspapers, and now I heard his friends and associates call him Billy.

"No," he told me after a second. "No, I don't prefer Billy. Cal calls me Billy, my mom calls me Billy, but no, I don't prefer to be called Billy." We settled on Bill, but so far as I can tell, it hasn't taken off.

The reporters who covered the league were good sources as well as good guests—informed speculation can be a very helpful commodity—but our jobs were very different. Play by play is not journalism. The fundamental principles of fairness and accuracy are the same, but I was paid by the team and promotion was an important element of my job: "There are plenty of good seats still available, so come on out the Churchville Road and make your plans now for the big series coming up when the first-place Atlantic City Surf come to Thomas Run Park." It was my job to portray the team in as positive a light as possible. I had no problems with that. Frankly, after a professional life on the sidelines, it was great to be openly *for* something. I didn't root for the team on the air—"C'mon, Danny, get a hit"—but there could be no doubt about which side I wanted to see win.

I did try to be careful about the word "we." Since I worked for the team, I could and did use it in the corporate sense: "We'd sure like you to join us . . ." I was a member of the traveling party, so after the game "we" would get on the bus. But I was most definitely not a player. "We" didn't hit home runs or strike out, "they" did; "we" were not five and a half games out of first place, Aberdeen was.

Part of my promotional job was to make the ballplayers look good. I have to say that I've never met a group of people as suspicious of the media, not even in the bowels of the Pentagon. If given a chance, I tried to explain that they should regard the Arsenal pregame show as training. If they ever achieved their ambition and made it to the big leagues, they might face some questions a little tougher than my waist-high fastballs. For example, I never invited players on the show until they had done something good to talk about. There were stretches of the season when this policy left me with nobody to talk to, at least not in the Arsenal dugout, but you never want to start an interview with "Gee, that was a tough one for you last night. . . ."

Some of the Spanish speakers didn't trust their English, and some claimed they didn't. More than a few of the others were afraid of the mike, and the one time I asked pitcher Eric Olszewski to come on the show, he looked at me as if I were trying to steal his soul. Some guys, bless their hearts, got it. Danny Perez was always willing to talk and Alex Andreopoulos was funny and articulate, but I think I had the most fun with Liam Healy. Liam was the kid of the team, a utility player who could get by on a miserly salary because he lived at home. Shy, almost stammering the first time out, it was hard to get him to say enough to fill out four minutes. By the end of the season, he was one of the best interviews on the team, ready to jab with me and swap stories.

I saved Johnny Isom until I really needed him. Johnny may be the nicest person on the planet, gentle, kind and quietly religious, a team leader and the guy you'd most like to have next to you in a foxhole. I'd known him as a Baysox and he gave me a big hello my first day up at Thomas Run Park. At that time, friendly faces were in short supply and I was grateful. At the start of the year, he was the one guy I could interview without preparation: I already knew that he'd grown up in Dallas where he was a star punter for his high school football team, and I knew his history in the Orioles organization.

One day, we got to the ballpark late in Somerset, I hadn't prepared an interview, so I tapped Johnny. "So," he asked as I set up my equipment, "somebody said you used to broadcast games in Bowie?"

Wow. I guess I'd made a big impression, huh?

After I thought about that for a while, it made sense. I'd been a part-timer, a peripheral figure in the clubhouse and a fellow traveler on the Baysox bus for just a couple of trips a couple of years ago. Ballplayers meet a zillion people every day and if they're as nice as Johnny, they shake hands, nod pleasantly and move on. Fans, sponsors, reporters, photographers. There were probably a few former teammates he wouldn't recognize anymore. In my other life, I've been in this situation, too. I've looked blankly at so many people I'd already been introduced to that I've long since switched from "Nice to meet you" to the ambiguous but safer "Good to see you."

It was also one of those moments I could bear in mind whenever I got a little carried away with my hemi-demi-semi celebrity. My correspondence was another way to check my ego. Every day on the pregame show, and sometimes during the game itself, I gave out addresses for letters and e-mail and asked listeners to send along any comments or questions they might have for me, for Darrell or for any of the ballplayers. I thought this would be a great way to engage the fans and kill a little airtime.

A couple of weeks into the season, I got a very polite e-mail from a man from Bel Air who said some nice things about the broadcasts and questioned my usage of "Arsenal" as a plural. I read it on the air during a game and explained that I used the team name as a plural to be consistent with "Orioles" or "Yankees," even though I knew that to be grammatically incorrect. It just sounded right, or less wrong. I didn't expect a flood of letters to follow, but a stream didn't seem to be too much to hope for.

That was the one and only communication from the WHFC audience all year. There was only one possible explanation. Nobody was listening.

Once, we tried to give away tickets on the air: "Be the fourth caller, and you'll receive a family four-pack . . ." Gary Helton took the calls back at the station and announced the name of the lucky winner during the next half-inning break.

"Hey, that went pretty well," I called to enthuse.

"That was my brother-in-law."

"You can't give away tickets to your family!"

"I don't plan to. That was just the first name I could think of."

"He wasn't the fourth caller?"

"He wasn't the first caller."

We retired the giveaway contest for a while. Later, another board op convinced Gary to try it again, and it worked, so maybe we picked up some listeners over the course of the season.

The core listening audience consisted of host families, the Arsenal front office and ballplayers' friends and relatives. One night when Matt Bacon was pitching, I mentioned that his wife was an athlete, too, a collegiate swimmer, who was back home rehabbing a shoulder injury. The next day on the bus, Matt leaned over and said, "I heard you were talking about my personal life."

Puzzled, I told him what I'd said, which didn't seem to reveal any dark secrets.

"Yeah, well, okay, I just don't want you talking about my wife, you know? I don't like to put my personal life out there."

Ah. I glanced over to notice that he didn't wear a ring, either.

In midseason, I moved out of the trailer at Thomas Run Park and started to work on the roof whenever the weather allowed. It was a pain to schlep all the equipment up and down the ladder before and after every game and it was sometimes difficult to get scoring decisions from the press box, but this became my realm. The view was fabulous. For one thing, I could see the left-field foul line for the first time, but that was the least of it. I could describe the traffic on Churchville Road and speak authoritatively on the availability of good parking. The press box faced east, so I'd never seen the sunset before. I could see weather develop and talk about activities on the softball fields that adjoin our diamond.

Many nights, the crowds were so small that I could hear conversations at home plate. One night, the guys in the press box counted sixteen fans in the stands as the second game of a doubleheader against the Bears ran very late. With Ozzie Canseco up at the plate, Julien Tucker buzzed a fastball and he let it go by.

"Stree-ah!" Umpire Joe Cruz pumped his right arm and called strike three.

"Joe!" Canseco's high voice was piping with outrage. "That pitch hasn't been a strike all night long!"

"Hey," Cruz came back, "it hasn't been 11:20 all night long, either."

A couple of innings later, Canseco came up again.

"Oz," Cruz told him, "that pitch last time might have been a little bit outside. But," he added, tugging on his mask, "it's now 11:45."

I found my note up on that roof. Noah Adams, who's been in radio even longer than I have, says that everybody has a place where their voice sounds right, where it's comfortable and resonant. Nervous beginners use what singers call a head voice, which is easier to control but higher pitched and generally less musical. Over time, you learn to relax and drop your voice into your chest. With more experience, you can hit the same note every time. After thirty years in the broadcast business, I thought I had it, but to my surprise, I found a much warmer spot up on the roof. That was a by-product of being on the air three hours every day and it's possible that I didn't find a better spot, just wore it in properly. Early in the season, the job was so tiring that I rooted for rain just to get a day off. Now, I couldn't wait for the game to begin and resented any weather that disrupted my rhythm. I knew as much about the league and its players as anyone, I learned to anticipate the order in which Rick preferred to use his relievers, and when Darrell would tell his outfield to play deep. I had command of my material and I never sounded so good in my life.

When the game was over, I stayed on for a five-minute wrap-up show, gave it back to the studio and packed up my stuff. It took four trips to carry the equipment and my score books down to the trailer and by the time I was ready to leave, Charlie Vascellaro and the grounds crew were the only people left.

I changed into a T-shirt and shorts in one of the Porta-Potties, unlocked my bike, flicked on the headlamp and the red rear flasher and punched my stopwatch as I rolled through the gate.

The first part of the trip home was a little scary because of the traffic on the highway and at that time of night, the bars were beginning to empty out. Negotiating the traffic light in Churchville could be tricky, but once I turned off at the Arctic Circle, I almost always had the back road to myself. Streetlights were few and far between, but I could spot the headlights of any cars from a long way off and I came to believe that it was safer to ride at night. Beyond the lights of the ballpark and the neon on the highway, the moon and the stars lit my way. The rotating beacon at the Harford County Airport gave me ample warning to slow down for my turns.

It was always faster on the way home. The route was a bit more downhill than up this direction, and I picked up some serious time right at the end. The hill that had been such a struggle in the heat and humidity of the afternoon was an exhilarating free fall in the cool of the night. After the last turn, one last little push, then I stopped pedaling and howled down through the dark.

8

ATLANTIC LEAGUE STANDINGS						
THROUGH GAMES OF JULY 10 (END OF FIRST HALF)						
NORTH DIVISION	W	L	PCT.	GB	STREAK	LAST 10
Nashua*	44	26	.629	—	L 1	8–2
Long Island	40	30	.571	4.0	W 4	9–1
Newark	38	32	.543	6.0	W 2	8–2
Bridgeport	35	35	.500	9.0	W 1	5–5
SOUTH DIVISION						
Somerset*	38	32	.543	—	L 2	5–5
Aberdeen	30	40	.429	8.0	W 2	3–7
Atlantic City	29	41	.414	9.0	L 1	2–8
Lehigh Valley	26	44	.371	12.0	W 2	3–7

*Won first half.

*T*he midsummer sun is just beginning to warm EAB Park on a clear Sunday morning. A few of the pitchers are getting their running in, some slowly jogging all the way around the warning track, others sprinting from foul pole to foul pole along the curve of the outfield fence. In the stands, workers blast the hardened mustard from last night's game off the dark green seats with high-pressure hoses powered by loud portable pumps. A tall man with moussed blond hair points out a puddle of spilled beer to one of the workers as he walks down the concrete steps and opens the gate next to the dugout. I half expect Frank Boulton to strike a master-of-all-he-surveys pose, but instead he grabs a gap-toothed rake and starts to clean up some wind-blown litter that's collected near the first-base stands.

This is the brand-new ballpark of the other expansion team in the Atlantic League this season, the Long Island Ducks. The landscaping outside the stadium isn't quite finished yet, but Frank Boulton's baby is in business. A little more than a year ago, this was an empty lot next to an abandoned state mental institution and across the street from Suffolk County's new court complex in Central Islip. Here in deepest suburbia, an hour and a quarter commute from Manhattan on the Long Island Railroad, Frank Boulton is perfectly placed to stick his success right in the eye of organized baseball.

Twenty years ago, it looked as if minor league baseball was about to shrivel and die. The once-booming network of more than five hundred teams in the days after the Second World War dwindled by more than half, ruined by competition from major league expansion, television and changing times. Not one franchise survived in New Jersey, for example, the most densely populated state in the union. Why would anybody pay to watch a bunch of unknown kids when they could take a quick drive into New York City or Philadelphia, or turn on a TV and see big-leaguers for nothing? Minor league ball-parks were mostly old and uncomfortable, out of the way and out of tune.

Frank Boulton is one of a new generation of owners who

believed that minor league baseball could not only survive, but thrive. In 1992 he bought a team then known as the Peninsula Pilots in Hampton, Virginia. "This was arguably the worst team in all of minor league baseball," he told me as we sat together near the first-base dugout. "The ballpark was so old, it still had blacks-only bathrooms.

"Well, we moved the team to Wilmington, Delaware, into a brand-new facility in '93, and the Wilmington Blue Rocks actually got voted one of the better teams in all of minor league baseball." Boulton and other innovators believed that minor league baseball could offer customers an unbeatable combination of price and value, but it had to be marketed properly. Good ballparks were the key. "At the root of this," he says, "is affordable family entertainment. You've heard that a lot as a kind of buzzword in minor league baseball, but it's true." Boulton raised his right arm to show off EAB Park as an example. "People can come out here and they get in for any-where between five and nine dollars, there are dollar hot dogs and dollar sodas available for the kids and they get entertained on the field and in between innings." There are also local microbrews and imported beers available for the parents, a full range of caps and shirts and souvenirs available in a well-stocked store, free parking, a first-class public address system and a large and impressive scoreboard out beyond the left-center-field fence. Peter Kirk of Maryland Baseball, another of minor league baseball's reinventors, put carousels and play-grounds in all of his parks. "Minor league baseball, as a cottage industry if you will, has done a very, very good job of enter-taining people and in building new facilities that have major league amenities on a minor league scale, where fans feel close to the action," Boulton said. "It's just the right chemistry."

Attendance, though, is just part of the formula. "A minor

league team can't survive on the turnstiles alone," says Peter Kirk, "no matter how good the attendance is. You have to have support from local businesses to subsidize the ticket prices."

The most important corporate support in EAB and the other new parks is the tier of skyboxes, fully catered suites where a CEO can entertain friends, employees and customers. They can enjoy the game inside in plush chairs in air-conditioned comfort, or sit outside, with every chance to catch a foul pop.

The other big engine of corporate largesse is ballpark advertising, called "signage." Like most minor league parks, the outfield fence at EAB is covered with plywood billboards eight feet high. Two more levels of ads just as big line a second fence that rises ten or fifteen feet beyond. Only dead center field, the area known as the "batter's eye," is blank. League rules require a solid, dark background to give hitters a chance to see the ball coming out of the pitcher's hand. In EAB Park, the batter's eye is the exact same shade of green as a bottle of Heineken and the beer company has paid to have its trademark red stars painted along the bottom. More sophisticated and more expensive ads are on the electronic scoreboard. At EAB, they even sold space on the foul poles.

In a lot of places, minor league teams adopted zany nicknames and splashy logos. "They invent animals to name teams after," Boulton laughed. "In our league, we'll have a new team next year called the Riversharks, and someone asked me, 'Is that a real thing, a rivershark?' and I said, 'Does it matter?' The logos, the marketing, the sports apparel, that's all a big part of it." This team is called the Long Island Ducks after a fondly remembered minor league hockey team that was, in turn, named after the most famous product of the local poultry industry. The team has caps and shirts with distinct color schemes for home and road games and a separate Sunday uniform as well, and of course, all the variants are available for sale in the busy gift shop. The cuddly, seven-foot-tall mascot, QuackerJack, waddles through the stands, pauses for pictures and hugs with the kids, every one of them blowing on a three-dollar yellow plastic kazoo shaped like a duck's bill, called a quacker.

Since the Ducks players are largely unknown, Frank Boulton has integrated his manager into the sales plan. The skipper is a local demigod, Bud Harrelson, a feisty shortstop in his playing days, the spark plug of the 1969 Miracle Mets and, later, the manager of the team. Harrelson has been in business with Boulton going back to the Peninsula Pilots and owns 25 percent of the Ducks.

"I'm from California originally, but I've lived here for more than thirty years now." Harrelson watches fielding practice as we chat in the dugout. "This is my community and it's nice to come out and entertain my friends and neighbors."

Harrelson is an intense and sometimes testy man, one of those managers who looks as if he hates his job. He can't hide his pain when his players make mistakes, and the deep lines under his eyes suggest that he debates his own decisions late into the night with a bottle of Maalox. He is honest enough to admit that his enthusiasm for managing is limited. He also knows that his name and his presence in uniform are critical to market the Ducks. "Whatever people are going to remember about me, whether it's the Pete Rose fight [a famous dustup in the 1972 National League playoffs] or the '69 Mets, I think eventually they're going to remember me and my partner Frank Boulton for bringing the first minor league franchise to Suffolk County, Long Island."

And the fans love it. On his way into the park with two kids,

Ken Feldman from Stony Brook tells me, "It's a great field, great game, great players and a great price!" He pauses, then adds, "It's also local, you know? Close to home. We can see the game and be home in bed for the eleven o'clock news." Bob Sidanko from West Islip picks up on the point: "It's great to have a local team, it's easy to get here, it's easy to park, the prices are very reasonable, it's just a fantastic venue." Sidanko and his wife, Lynn, are season-ticket holders. "I absolutely love it," she says, "you really get to know the players, and you know they're not making a lot of money, that they're here for the love of the game." Allen Zarrow has come out from Brooklyn, even though the Mets are playing at home today. "It's pure family fun, I know that sounds like a commercial, but it really is. It's the way baseball used to be."

The first few weeks of the season, the Ducks pull in more than five thousand fans a game and once school lets out, they sell out every night. By the time the season's over, the average attendance is higher than EAB's seating capacity of just over six thousand. It is one of baseball's greatest success stories of 2000.

It was supposed to happen in 1995.

In addition to the team in Wilmington, Boulton and his partners also owned the Albany-Colonie Yankees, a team in the Double A Eastern League that he wanted to relocate to his hometown. "In 1993, 1994, I petitioned the Eastern League and the National Association [the National Association of Professional Baseball is the umbrella for affiliated minor league teams] to move the franchise here to Long Island. We got the funding to build a ballpark, the National Association approved the move and we were all set to go, but then the New York Mets filed a complaint."

This happened at a curious moment in baseball history. The major league owners had just fired Fay Vincent, so there was no commissioner of baseball. In that situation, the professional baseball agreement, the deal that brings the major and minor leagues under the jurisdiction of the commissioner, calls for the creation of a special fourteen-member committee: the presidents of the two major leagues, ten major league owners and four minor league owners. Peter Kirk of Maryland Baseball was one of the minor league owners on this Executive Council. "There were a lot of lively debates," he told me. "I still laugh at the idea that I was once a one-fourteenth commissioner. It was a joke, because the votes were always 10–4."

At the time, minor league teams were barred from building a ballpark within thirty-five miles of an established minor league team, measured from home plate to home plate. Major League Baseball's territorial rules were vague enough to allow teams to share the New York, Chicago and Los Angeles markets, but appeared to prohibit competition within fifteen miles.

"I knew the rules," Boulton says, "so I go to the meeting with a Hagstrom map and a ruler. Now, I knew that the Hagstrom family had been in the map business for a long time and the ruler came from my contractor who had just built an addition onto my house, so I knew that was accurate." His proposed park in Suffolk County qualified no matter which mileage standard applied, but he did not count on the rivalry between the two local major league teams. Mets owner Fred Wilpon did not see a minor league team that wanted to operate on the fringe of his market, but an invasion of Long Island by Yankees owner George Steinbrenner.

Peter Kirk says the Mets never used the word "territory" because they didn't have a leg to stand on. "They talked about protecting their market. They thought a minor league team would hurt their market and especially a Yankees minor league team. The major league owners were all concerned about encroachment. The minor league owners said, Look, we have an agreement here, there are rules and this clearly falls within the rules, it's been properly approved by the Eastern League and the National Association, all the procedures were followed, so what's the problem?"

The only way the Executive Council could go outside the rules was to invoke a catchall clause: "the best interests of baseball." Kirk says the minor league owners on the committee argued that the best interests of baseball and the best interests of the New York Mets were not necessarily identical.

"All of this took a fair amount of time to talk about, and this wasn't the biggest deal in the world for some of the major league owners and a few of them fell asleep," Kirk reported. "Frank was invited to come in to make his presentation. They listened politely, Frank left and the vote was called.

"At that point, one of the owners who'd been sleeping woke up and said, 'I'm confused. What are we voting on?' And Steve Greenberg [then the counsel to the commissioner's office] said, 'Let me make it simple for you. A "yes" vote is for George Steinbrenner and a "no" vote is for Fred Wilpon.' And they all went with Fred Wilpon. It was 10–4, just like all the other votes."

When he heard the verdict, Boulton spluttered. "My whole project was reduced to a popularity contest!"

Major league baseball was able to enforce its will on Boulton because of the game's famous antitrust exemption. The Supreme Court ruled in the 1920s that baseball could operate as a monopoly because it was a sport, rather than a business. "One would wonder," Boulton asked rhetorically, "if Major League Baseball didn't abuse the antitrust exemption. I got calls from people, elected officials, and it would have been very easy for me to go down to Washington to testify against the exemption. A lot of people, Senator Howard Metzenbaum in particular, wanted me to testify. I did not. I don't want to hurt baseball on any level, from Little League to the major leagues, so I went and testified in favor of the exemption. But"—and he pauses for emphasis—"it is, or it should be, a privilege and not a right."

The Atlantic League was born at the Executive Council meeting, with Fred Wilpon as an unlikely midwife.

Independent baseball leagues began to reemerge over the past ten years because there was demand. Each major league team has no more than seven minor league affiliates and most have six, which leaves more cities and towns that want professional baseball than the fixed number of teams available. In Minnesota, the Saint Paul Saints of the Northern League proved that independents could thrive even in the shadow of a major league ballpark, but most of the Northern League teams were in small, isolated communities. The other independent leagues were even smaller, and many knowledgeable executives questioned whether the idea could work back east. It was the New Jersey problem all over again.

Part of the answer arrived in 1994, when the Eastern League moved a team into a brand-new ballpark on the Delaware River in Trenton. The runaway success of the Trenton Thunder convinced the baseball entrepreneurs and local officials. Minor league parks could revive small downtowns the same way that Oriole Park at Camden Yards cemented the redevelopment of Baltimore's Inner Harbor. Within five years, independent teams were playing in Newark, Atlantic City, Bridgewater and Montclair, another park was rising in Camden (the future home of the Riversharks) and there was talk of a team for Hackensack. "There were a lot of people who didn't think we could make this economically viable on an independent level," Frank Boulton says, "and while there are still challenges, I think we've proven that that's a reality."

Few of the new independent teams did as well as the Ducks and a couple could fairly be described as struggling, but the concept worked well enough that both of New York's major league teams decided to jump on the bandwagon. The Yankees moved a rookie league team that they own to Staten Island and the Mets did the same in Brooklyn.

"I don't know if 'ironic' is the right word," Frank Boulton says, "but, yes, I find that very interesting." He leans back and smiles. "At the end of the day, though, I'm really happy the way it happened. I talk to Peter Kirk and we often shake our heads about it and smile. Even though it's seven years later, at the end of the day, what we have is an unbelievable development here in the Atlantic League."

A league of their own.

Atlantic League marketers like to describe the level of play in the league as Quadruple A, suggesting that its players are better than those at the highest level of the affiliated minors. This is simply not true, but to dismiss them as a bunch of castoffs and rejects isn't right, either. The consensus is that the pitching in the Atlantic League is roughly equivalent to Double A, the hitting to Triple A. And there are two special categories of players in the league that may soon make that Quadruple A label more accurate: draft dodgers and pinch hitters.

Bobby Hill was an all-American at a big-time baseball school, the University of Miami. A lightning-fast switch-hitting middle infielder who hit for both power and average, Hill was one of the top prospects in the draft. When he signed with agent Scott Boras, a notoriously difficult negotiator, major league teams knew that he would be a very expensive commodity. Because of that, Hill slipped into the second round before the Chicago White Sox decided to take the plunge. The negotiations did not go well, so Boras and Hill decided to pull a J. D. Drew.

A couple of years earlier, the Phillies drafted Drew number one overall, but ran into problems with—no coincidence—agent Scott Boras. Unhappy with Philly's offer, Drew took out a multimillion-dollar insurance policy in case of injury and went to play for the Saint Paul Saints of the independent Northern League. Boras tried to argue that this made him a free agent, and if he'd prevailed, he could have auctioned the kid off to the highest bidder for maybe ten million dollars. It didn't work, but after a year of independent ball, Drew reentered the draft, and signed a very nice deal with St. Louis.

Spurning the White Sox, Bobby Hill came to play for the Newark Bears. The Atlantic League offered him high-quality competition and a showcase to display his skills. "It's been a real advantage for me," Hill said in the Bears dugout. "I could have stayed home and waited it out, but I wanted to show everybody that I was healthy, a hundred percent ready to play, and I think I learned more here than I would have in A ball down in the White Sox organization. I'm playing with veterans out there, learning the ins and outs of baseball on the field and off. I'm going to walk into an organization with one full season of professional baseball behind me and I'm going to know how to act like a professional."

In the 2000 draft, Hill was selected by the crosstown Chicago Cubs, but because of a subsequent shake-up in their front office, they didn't sign him right away. In effect, the Cubs seasoned their prospect in the Atlantic League.

Hill's Newark teammate Ozzie Canseco is at the other end of the spectrum in age and experience. Ozzie was converted into a pitcher in high school. "I had a very good arm, a live arm they called it. I wasn't allowed to hit all the way through high school, so Jose developed much more in that aspect, and I was drafted by the Yankees as a pitcher in the second round. I spent three and a half years in their organization, I got as high as the Florida State League, but I hurt my arm and I had to start my career all over again. I lost six and a half years' experience as a hitter, so I had a lot of catching up to do."

Ozzie made it up to the big leagues for a couple of cups of coffee, one with his twin's Oakland A's team in 1990, but strikeouts and injuries sent him back down again. He has all of Jose's great power, though, and this season, finally healthy, he hit so well in Newark that when word came in August that the New York Yankees had signed Canseco, more than a few people asked, "Which one?"

There is a small, select group of older players like Ozzie Canseco that no major league team wants, until they need them. In the early and middle parts of the season, they clutter up a major league roster and complain about the lack of playing time and are generally useless. In August and September, though, in a pennant race, every manager wants experienced guys to come off the bench late in a ball game, sure-handed infielders unfazed by pressure and big boppers to pinch-hit in the clutch. As Frank Boulton put it, "Ozzie Canseco might well be the twentieth- or twenty-fifth-best designated hitter in baseball, but there are only fourteen major league teams that use the DH. He's an older player you don't necessarily want on your Triple A team, and the Atlantic League is the perfect place for him to show what he can do and stay ready."

There is a very vocal element in organized baseball that wants to see the independents die. In response to the competition from new teams and new leagues, the National Association renamed itself. After decades of ducking what it regarded as a pejorative term, it has now officially trademarked the term "The Minor Leagues." The intention is to question the legitimacy of the independents and, if possible, to establish a distinction in the minds of the fans. "Some minor league owners somehow don't think of it as real baseball," says Peter Kirk. "They see it as a threat. There were a couple of owners in the Eastern League who felt so strongly that they wanted to bring me up on charges because I had an independent team at the same time that I had affiliated teams. Of course, there's nothing in the rules to prevent that, but they wanted to do it anyway."

Kirk argues that visceral opposition to independents makes no sense. "You have to remember that at one point or another, every league was an independent league. The whole structure we have now, where the major league affiliate supplies the entire roster of players, that's relatively new. That was different in the eighties. I was an owner back then and I would sign some of the players and the big-league team provided others." That's the way the Mexican League operates now, and many believe that it's only a matter of time before similar agreements are worked out on this side of the border. If big-league teams can work out a way to loan their prospects to independents, they might eliminate a level of the minors and save some money.

Even now, independents like Frank Boulton don't want to challenge baseball's monopoly. The Atlantic League has repeatedly applied to become part of the National Association, either as a full member or as an associate, on the same basis as the Mexican League. The opposition is so emotional that all efforts to explore the idea have been blocked. Peter Kirk sees this as self-defeating. "I'm reminded of the Ted Turner quote," he said, citing the former owner of the Atlanta Braves. "He said, 'We've got the only legal monopoly in the country and we're fucking it up.' Why should we have two completely different minor league systems operating under different sets of rules, when we could have one system, one set of rules that includes everybody?"

For a long time, affiliated teams marketed their relationship to the big club: "Come and see the Yankees/Dodgers/Mets stars of the future!" More and more, executives realized that this had limited appeal. While the Orioles have three minor league affiliates in Maryland, that's not typical. Most farm teams are a long way away from the fan base of the parent club. Even when they are nearby, affiliates do better marketing themselves as the hometown team. For example, when the Double A Canton/Akron Indians moved into a beautiful new ballpark in downtown Akron, they became the Akron Aeros despite the gravitational effect of the parent team in the same state. Major league clubs are increasingly reluctant to schedule in-season exhibitions against their minor league teams, which was both a big moneymaker for the locals and an important way to cement the relationship.

Peter Kirk and Maryland Baseball owned half of the Aberdeen venture. The other 50 percent was not interested in a challenge to organized baseball, or even in making big money out of the deal. The Ripken family wanted to build a memorial to Cal Ripken, Senior, who was a coach and manager in the Orioles system. Both Cal, Jr., and little brother Bill went to Aberdeen High School. Senior never played in the major leagues, but he was one of the architects of The Oriole Way, a philosophy that stressed execution and fundamentals and which spawned one of the most productive minor league organizations in baseball. His son and namesake is its most famous product. Senior was given an opportunity to manage in Baltimore when both Cal, Jr., and Bill Ripken were on the team, and his abrupt dismissal helped sour the family's relationship with the Orioles ownership. A baseball academy was Senior's idea: "Learn to Play the Right Way." Though listed as director of baseball operations for the Arsenal, Bill spent most of his time traveling to clinics around the country on Ripken Academy business. He, Cal, Jr., and especially their mother, Vi, wanted to establish a permanent legacy in their hometown.

Aberdeen, Maryland, is a small, gritty city about thirty miles northeast of Baltimore on I-95. The main drag is Philadelphia Boulevard, a grimy strip of diners, flophouses and muffler stores glimpsed by thousands every day from the windows of the Amtrak Metroliners that rattle the flimsy depot as they race between New York and D.C. Havre de Grace, the next town north, is a neat, prosperous community at the mouth of the Susquehanna River with a lovely waterfront, new condos and extensive marinas. Aberdeen's access to the Chesapeake is blocked by the U.S. Army's Aberdeen Proving Ground to the east of the railroad tracks. On a cloudy day, explosions echo up the rolling hills to the west. Once you get outside of town, across the interstate, horse farms dot the countryside next to fields of Silver Queen corn. Aberdeen proper has two claims to fame: the Ordnance Museum on the army base and the Ripken Museum downtown.

On the grounds of City Hall, right next to the museum, Cal Ripken, Junior, is immortalized in bronze. The curious chocolate-colored statue greets you as you get off the train. Other than the fact that it exists, it is not especially flattering. The baseball immortal stands there hatless in rumpled double knits, right arm extended in an awkward-looking welcome. There is no team logo or Orioles black-and-orange, no number 8 on the back of the uniform, perhaps to protect against the outside chance that Cal might someday play for another team or wear another number. The sculptor has not repaired the hero's receding hairline or covered his bald spot. It's a modest representation of, by all accounts, a modest man.

Late in his baseball life, Cal, Junior, decided to do something incontrovertibly right for his hometown. The baseball academy is to be a complex of six small fields modeled after famous big league parks—a miniature Fenway Park, Wrigley Field, Yankee Stadium, and Ebbets Field would stand next to youth-size copies of Baltimore's old Memorial Stadium and new Camden Yards. The facility, including dormitories and offices, would also be the permanent home of the Babe Ruth League. Hundreds of thousands of kids play Babe Ruth–League ball around the country. The 12- to 14-year-old age group is already named the Cal Ripken, Junior, Division and the establishment of the league's annual tournament in Aberdeen would make this city a regular stop on the amateur baseball circuit. It would take its place with Williamsport, Pennsylvania, host to the Little League World Series, and Omaha, Nebraska, the home of the College World Series.

A professional baseball team for Aberdeen was a separate project developed by Peter Kirk and Maryland Baseball, but serendipity demanded a merger. Ripken Stadium would be the team's new home and the centerpiece of the Ripken Academy complex. The Tufton Group, which handles Cal, Junior's investments, would provide nine million dollars to build the academy and for the right to name the stadium. Maryland Baseball put up two million more, with the rest of the twenty-five-million-dollar total to come from the city of Aberdeen, Harford County and the state of Maryland. A lot of the expense involved infrastructure, including a new exit ramp off I-95 to service the ballpark and the extension of water and sewer lines underneath the interstate.

In late January 2000, Cal and Governor Parris Glendening presided over a news conference at the state capitol in Annapolis to announce that the deal was done. The Maryland legislature had agreed to seven million dollars over the next three years; local authorities committed to seven million more. The business plan projected that the stadium/academy complex would create 430 jobs and generate twenty-six million dollars in revenue per year. The facility would also attract a hotel, a high-tech gym, restaurants and other businesses to an undeveloped neighborhood that carried none of the baggage of downtown Aberdeen.

There are always some reluctant fits in these financial puzzles, but the last big piece was to enlist the support of the local business community. The marketing staff began to approach companies to make long-term agreements to rent luxury boxes and advertising space on the scoreboard and the outfield fence. Once there were enough commitments, those contracts could be leveraged into loans to fund construction of the ballpark.

From the beginning, there were questions about the size and prosperity of the market; Aberdeen is a relatively small and scuffling city. Havre de Grace is much better off, Bel Air is booming and there is a ring of well-heeled smaller suburbs on this northern edge of Baltimore. A ballpark site with access from I-95, the glittering prospect of a brand-new facility and the magic of the Ripken name would all ensure community support. Ripken Stadium would be ready to host the Aberdeen Arsenal in 2001.

The Atlantic League was on a different timetable. The Long Island Ducks were ready to play now. Any league's schedule demands an even number of teams—an odd number means that somebody has to be idle every day—so the choice was either to shut down the still-troubled Lehigh Valley franchise for a year or to get Aberdeen to come in a year early. Prudence had few backers. The league wanted to sustain its momentum and lay the groundwork for more expansion in the years to come. Lehigh Valley would struggle on, and Aberdeen was in.

Which meant the new team needed to find a field. The fall-back option was to play home games at Delmarva, Frederick or Bowie while the Shorebirds, Keys or Baysox were on the road. Thomas Run Park was a greatly inferior facility but a much better plan. The community-college field needed a new infield, bullpens, seats, bathrooms, concession stands and a press box, all of which cost money, but it had lights, a primitive scoreboard and, most important, it had location. It was just six miles away from the new stadium site, so any fan base that developed would transfer easily to the new ballpark. The team would be able to generate coverage in the local newspapers, get its games on the radio and begin to establish roots in the community.

Just before the season started, some of the Arsenal's new neighbors complained of plans to sell beer at the ballpark, because an elementary school and a church were nearby. Beer is one of the financial staples of baseball. Teams not only make big profits on every cupful, they attract more customers, young men who might otherwise spend their summer evenings at the local bar. The team pointed out that there was already a liquor store and a bar nearby as well, but decided not to fight too hard. Goodwill for the seasons to come was more important than beer sales this year. The partners knew going in that they would lose money the first season; the beer ban guaranteed that they would lose a lot of money. Peter Kirk said, "We took one for the league." Keith Lupton told me that they lost half a million dollars before the first pitch was thrown.

By this point in the season, we might have picked up a few more listeners on the radio, but attendance at Thomas Run Park continued at a trickle. The date to break ground for Ripken Stadium had been pushed back twice. Optimists speculated that the new ballpark would be ready by the middle of the 2001 season, and pessimists began to question whether this project was going to survive.

On the team's only home stand in the month of July, Keith arranged a tribute to Aberdeen's only other professional baseball team, the Canners, a club that played in the Susquehanna League right after the Second World War. The 2000 Arsenal score book featured a 1946 Canners team picture on the cover that included three Ripkens: Bill, Ollie and Cal, Senior, who was the batboy. Ominously, the Canners had not lasted long. Charlie Vascellaro dug up a copy of a poem published in the sports section of a local newspaper, the *Democrat*, in 1955.

ODE TO THE CANNERS
Whatever became of their friends and their pals
of short years ago, those fine fellows and gals?

Those fans that rooted and hollered for every great play,
Those bleachers that were crowded, happy and gay?
Oh, where are they now, those fans that once cared?
For the Aberdeen bleachers lay deserted and bared.
Then the season was over, the tough race it was run,
With the Susky League pennant conceded and won.
When unloved and unwanted, our gallants went down
In the post season playoffs at old Chesapeake town.
Now is there an Aberdeen fan who is heartsick and sore
O'er the plight of the Canners, who were game to the core?
Or are we so calloused that our voices are stilled
Caring naught for the Canners nor the traditions we've
    killed?
For there were Jacobs and Baldwin and the three Ripkens,
    too,
Ferrell, Clessauras and Walker all in there fighting for you.
While Grafton and Trago were the stout armed pair
Who hurled out their arms, but you didn't care.
So whatever became of their friends and their pals
Of short years ago, those fine fellows and gals.

9

ATLANTIC LEAGUE STANDINGS						
THROUGH GAMES OF JULY 30*						
NORTH DIVISION	W	L	PCT.	GB	STREAK	LAST 10
Bridgeport	10	6	.625	—	W 5	6–4
Nashua**	9	7	.563	1.0	L 4	4–6
Long Island	8	9	.471	2.5	L 3	4–6
Newark	7	8	.467	2.5	W 6	6–4
SOUTH DIVISION						
Atlantic City	9	6	.600	—	W 1	6–4
Lehigh Valley	7	9	.438	2.5	L 3	5–5
Aberdeen	6	8	.429	2.5	W 2	4–6
Somerset**	7	10	.412	3.0	L 1	4–6

*Please note that these standings reflect the beginning of a new season.
**Won first half.

*A*n hour before game time, Perry Barber sits on a folding chair in front of the umpires' shack at Thomas Run Park, dips two fingers into a can of mud and rubs the muck onto a brand-new Atlantic League baseball. Her right and left hand alternate as she rotates the ball to make sure of a nice, even, light brown coating. Three twists per hand, and the ball is almost dry as she flips it into a canvas bag. She'll smear three dozen baseballs before she's done. Over the next couple of hours, they will be fouled off and thrown in the dirt, take flight over the outfield fence and enter the record book as groundouts and pop flies, as ball four and strike three.

The purpose of the mud is to remove the slick sheen that newly minted baseballs acquire in the Rawlings factory, but Barber, a student of the game, admits she doesn't know why umpires got stuck with the chore of rubbing them up.

"I know old-time managers like Connie Mack and John McGraw used to play tricks with the balls before the game started." Her blond hair is pinned to fit beneath the blue umpire's cap. "They would freeze them, do things to them that were undetectable, to help their teams out."

When I suggest that umpires might be the only ones trusted with the balls before the game, she laughs.

"Yeah, because we're so trustworthy and diligent, and because it's a dirty job and maybe nobody else wants to do it."

Perry Barber is the girl my mother wanted me to marry. She's smart, attractive and rich. Her father inherited the Barber Steamship Company and her mother was an actress who worked on radio soap operas and played Winnie the Wave in a U.S. Navy recruiting campaign. In the mid-sixties, Perry and I both lived on the East Side of Manhattan and went to fancy private schools, though most would rate her Miss Hewitt's School for Girls as a cut above my Riverdale Country School. In an effort to educate me in the social graces of the class to which she aspired, my mother packed me off to the debutante balls where young ladies like Perry Barber were formally introduced to society.

My mother grew up in a working-class Irish family in Jersey City during the Depression and saw herself as Rose Kennedy. Her plan for me and the nice girl I would meet called for Ivy League/Seven Sisters educations and a grand wedding. I would go into my father's trade, medicine, or maybe banking or law, while she would raise the kids and we would all summer on Martha's Vineyard. In this, as in so many things, my mother would be disappointed. Instead of sweeping a debutante off her feet, I spent my time at the cotillions in dark corners hiding my pimples. If Perry and I met, I don't remember. I'm a couple of years older, so probably not.

Instead of Princeton, I hung out at a hippie radio station in New York City where I hoped to meet girls. I badly overestimated the glamour factor of a life behind the mike. Like sports and comic books and science fiction, my other fave raves at the time, Free Form radio turned out to be mostly a guy thing. Or maybe it was me.

But, again, I might easily have met Perry Barber. She went to Columbia, but dropped out of her parents' social circle to become a singer/songwriter. The folk scene in New York wasn't all *that* big. When she told me that Richie Havens got her a job at the Cafe Wha in Greenwich Village, about opening for Hall and Oates and Bruce Springsteen and Billy Joel, I thought we must have run into each other. She almost certainly heard me on the radio, I probably heard her perform, we undoubtedly had friends in common, but nobody remembers. The sixties bled into the seventies and our lives diverged. Thirty years later we finally met in baseball.

Perry Barber is executive assistant to Joe Klein, who is, in turn, executive director of the Atlantic League, the guy whose signature she's smudging on those baseballs. She schedules the umpires, makes sure that a crew is assigned to each game and takes care of hotel reservations and the other logistical details. If somebody's sick or injured, if the emergency backup can't make it, she gets to do what she really likes. She puts on a uniform, a chest protector and a mask, and goes out to call balls and strikes.

Baseball entered Perry Barber's life obliquely. She loved to play trivia. She loved the snappy competition and appeared twice as a contestant on *Jeopardy!*—once when she was nineteen on the old Art Fleming version, then again later with Alex Trebek. In an effort to get a better command over one of her weakest areas, she went to a bookstore and came home with Roger Angell's *Five Seasons*, *Eight Men Out* by Eliot Asinof and a collection of Ring Lardner's *You Know Me Al* stories.

"I started to learn about the history of baseball and the anecdotes, but at the time I thought of it as history, not as a game." Charmed by Jimmy Breslin's *Can't Anyone Here Play This Game?*, she started going out to Shea Stadium with her sister to see the Mets. What started as an amusement developed into an interest and then edged toward passion.

"When we could, we'd follow the Mets on the road. I was lucky enough to have family in Saint Louis and San Francisco and in Southern California. I remember once in San Diego, I saw Tom Seaver throw over to first base seventeen times in a row trying to hold Alan Wiggins on base, and he stole second anyway." She was visiting her mother in Indio, California, when baseball went out on strike in 1981. "I was distraught that I couldn't see a game, and my mother saw an ad in the newspaper, looking for umpires for Little League. I think she was just trying to get me out of the house, but I thought it was terrific that my mom would even make the suggestion. That's not what daughters did when she grew up. Not exactly Miss Hewitt's."

Perry went down to the league office and lied about her credentials and talked her way into the job. "I didn't have a proper uniform, I was just wearing black pants from JCPenney and a light blue shirt. I had a bubble chest protector and I borrowed a mask from somewhere. I certainly didn't look very professional."

In her second game, there was an incident she describes as a watershed. "I walked out on the field full of hope and promise, I was all excited about being an umpire and getting out there and doing this and finding something that I liked so much, and the manager of this team of eight-year-old boys takes one look at me, and starts screaming, 'Hey, let's go, let's get out of here. We're not going to play if *she's* umpiring.'

"Up until that point, I'd always been one of those people who wanted to please people. I was brought up to be winning and charming, I went to a private school and I was never taught to be . . . assertive, shall we say. But at that moment it occurred to me, if I let this guy do this, those kids aren't going to play. That was why we were all there, so the kids can play and have fun. Why he would inflict his attitude toward me on them confused me, so I went over to him and did something I usually didn't do. I said, 'Look, I've been hired by the league and if you have any complaints, go to the league office after the game and get me fired.' And I said it really loud, so the kids' parents would hear me, I wasn't dumb. 'I think you should let the boys play, because that's what they're here for and whatever you feel about me, it's not fair to them that you don't want to play just because you don't want me to be the umpire.' And of course, the parents were looking on and thinking, 'I chauffeured little Tommy here from his dentist appointment, so what are you going to do, Mister Manager, I think she's right.'

"So we played the game. For me, that was an eye-opening experience. I was just amazed that I stood up for myself that way. That was something new for me."

That winter, she attended Harry Wendelstedt's umpire school in Daytona Beach, Florida. She was the only female student and discovered that she was behind the curve. She'd never played the game and she didn't know enough, beginning with the rules. Eventually, she went to umpire's school four times and her male colleagues now acknowledge her mastery of the rule book. "In twenty years, I've never made a mistake on the rules. No, wait. I remember I made a mistake once on an illegal substitution at a tournament in Florida. I love knotty problems and weird plays." But it was still tough to get a job.

"I umpired high school and college games in Florida, and I really cut my teeth in the Stan Musial Leagues on Long Island. This is for older guys, college age and up. They were amateurs and some of them were very poorly behaved, but because they didn't get paid, there was no mechanism to enforce the rules. You couldn't fine them and it was all so loosely organized that you couldn't suspend them or anything, so I learned to work with idiots."

Another place to work was the new fantasy camps, where middle-aged dreamers paid to shag flies with a few of their boyhood idols. The ex–major leaguers ran their lumpy charges through fielding and batting practice, and the long weekend culminated with a series of games. Perry started a business that supplied the umpiring crews. "People were happy to use me to make all the administrative arrangements, but I realized most people would not hire me as an umpire. Most of them hung up on me when I called, a woman umpire was a very hard sell. But I knew a lot of guys from umpire school, so I had the contacts. I hooked up with associations and that made it possible for me to assign myself to games." One of the fantasy camp operators she worked for was Bud Harrelson, who would later recommend her to Joe Klein and the Atlantic League.

Her recollection is that the pay was $12 per game in Little League, $35 in high school, college, $40–45, and $55 a game in the Stan Musial League. "I'm lucky. As an heiress, I've never had to depend on it. But honestly, I don't think anybody does it for the money. Obviously, a lot of the guys can use the extra income, but there are lots of ways they could be making more. They're out there for the same reason I am. Because we love it.

"You know that movie *Thelma and Louise*?" She leans back in her chair. "When they're in the T-bird driving toward the edge of the Grand Canyon, Geena Davis I think it is, she turns to Susan Sarandon and says, 'Are you awake?' 'Yes, I'm awake, I never remember feeling so awake!' Well, that's the way I feel out on the field. It's the same charge that movie stars and rock stars get, that good energy. As an umpire, I know that a lot of what I do is performance, within the parameters of professional conduct. It's so challenging, and it's something that was never prepared for me. I found this for myself."

She paused and took a breath. "When men told me I was terrible and that I ought to quit, it just made me determined to get better. I was always good in school, you know, class president, student council, honor roll. When I started as an umpire, I wasn't very good, but that didn't make me feel worthless. It made me determined and challenged and excited about being involved in something wonderful and magical. A woman my age has no realistic chance to make the major leagues and that's not my ambition. I'm not going to say I never thought about it, but not now. I've always gone where opportunities presented themselves, but there are realities, so the big time and the big money, that's not going to happen for me. It's the work that counts. It's the charge I get when I walk out on the ballfield."

Umpiring can be physically draining. "People have the impression that we stand around out there and move every once in a while and make calls, but, next time you're out at the game, take a look and you'll see that umpires are on the move every play if they're doing it right." It's even more demanding with a three-person crew, which is the standard in Double A, Triple A and the Atlantic League. Wild pitches and foul tips bite umpires everywhere. "I got a pretty good one here the other night," Perry said, pointing to a purple-and-yellow mark on her upper arm. "I've had several broken bones in my career. Bumps and bruises are part of the game, you get used to them. I call them my war wounds. This May, I had one on my leg that looked like the continent of Africa. I was proud of that one."

Absorbing as it is, the game lasts only about three hours. There is a lot of downtime. "I've heard"—Perry smiled—"that a lot of male umpires go out and get drunk and pick up women and chew tobacco and spit and curse and stay up late. Me? I usually go home and watch the news." The first part isn't the only exaggeration. A night owl going back to her days in rock and roll, she finds it hard to unwind after a game. "I check my e-mail and check to see what the other teams did that night, and I try to get into bed by two if I can, but it's not always easy. You have to have stamina and endurance to get used to the hours and it can be a pretty lonely life. Some people quit or get divorced or get drunk or whatever.

"My first husband got bored with it. I'm not the easiest person to live with, I'm compulsively neat, but the real problem was that I was never home weekends. He'd want to go out Saturday night and I had a doubleheader. But now I'm very lucky because the Atlantic League has teams up and down the East Coast. I live in New York City, so, unless the game is in Nashua or Aberdeen or Atlantic City I can drive home every night. I'm not leaving the field thinking, 'I'll go back to my room and get McDonald's and watch *SportsCenter* four times,' the way some of the guys do. I'm going home to a wonderful man who loves and supports me and thinks it's very cool when I come home and tell him about all the crazy things that happened that day."

Ballplayers have also questioned her career choice. "At the start, a lot of them assumed I was either a lesbian or looking for a husband, that I'm incapable of bearing children or having a successful relationship.

"My simplest explanation is that I do it because I love it, because I feel like I'm making an important contribution out there. For me, the issue has never been feminism or making a point, it's way more personal than that. I feel joy in it.

"That being said, I do hope some girls see me out there and start thinking that they might want to do this as well." Perry Barber is student enough to know that she is the fifth woman to call balls and strikes in a professional baseball game. "I'm just following in the path established by Pam Postema and the others.

"In Newark one night, a little girl came up to me and said, 'I want to be an umpire,' and I got such, such a good feeling." The wistful moment glistens into Perry Barber's quick laugh.

"But I wanted to tell her, Think about it seriously before you do it. It'll break your heart, but you'll be a stronger person for it. Stronger and happier."

Perry Barber is sinewy and strong, but she is not a large woman. Though the home-plate umpire's mask and armor bulk her up a bit, she's sometimes dwarfed by the hitter and catcher. Not a problem, she says. "I've always been small, so size doesn't faze me. Some guys assume I can't see over the catcher and get a good look at the strike zone, but that's just positioning, mechanics. You just line yourself up in the slot.

"There are some big guys in this league, though. You look at Nashua, I'm impressed by the size of some of those guys, but they don't intimidate me. I know people don't think of it this way, but ballplayers are so sensitive. You look at them cross-eyed, and they're convinced you're out to get them. They all think the umps are out to screw them, and you know, sometimes they're right. There are some umps who think they're bigger than the game, they exert their authority by making a spectacle of themselves and have to show everybody they're the boss. I think that's a mistake.

"Lots of people criticize me for being too lenient, they say I take too much abuse. Like when guys slam their helmets down or drop their bats. I ignore it. It makes them look like an idiot, not me, and besides, if I toss them, I have to fill out a lot of paperwork. You know, it's funny, sometimes, there's a bit of a contretemps and ballplayers run around and shout, 'Hey, you're supposed to control the game!' And I say to them, 'Look, I'm an umpire. I'm supposed to call ball/strike, fair/foul, I'm not supposed to be out here baby-sitting a bunch of overgrown two-year-olds throwing temper tantrums. You're supposed to be able to control yourself.'"

Perry was behind the plate for one big contretemps involving the Arsenal. Late in a game in Newark, Aberdeen reliever David Lundquist came in to protect a 2–1 lead. He got a strikeout and a ground ball for the first two outs, then worked the count to two balls and two strikes on Bears catcher Peto Ramirez. Expecting something off-speed, Ramirez watched, helpless, as Lundy's fastball hummed across at the knees. Perry called it a ball.

"I went ballistic," Lundquist told me later. "I mean, that pitch was right there, strike three, let's go home. I set the guy up and make the perfect pitch, the game's over, and I don't get the call. I never go after umpires," Lundquist said, shaking his head at the memory of his theatrics that night. "I just don't do it. I know it's hard and they all miss calls sometimes, but that one, I was ready to kill her. I don't think I've ever been so mad."

He let it affect him, too. Ramirez hit his next pitch for a homer to tie the game and the Bears scored four more runs before Lundquist finally got himself under control. I asked Lundy if he thought the fact that the umpire was a woman had anything to do with it, and he said he didn't think so. He did admit that he would have been better off if she'd thrown him out of the game for arguing balls and strikes.

Perry remembered the play just as clearly, except she thought the pitch was low. "I spoke to Joe [Klein] about the play and asked him what I should have done, and he said that in that situation, call it a strike and ring him up. A borderline pitch with the game on the line, he's got to be swinging. But I don't know," she added. "I don't know if I'd change the call if I had it to do over again. You've got to call them the way you see them."

A week or so later, after a game in Bridgeport, I was talking with Darrell in the Carousel Bar at the Holiday Inn when

Lundquist came up and offered to buy a round. The big right-handed reliever had joined the club in late June. Confident, well spoken and well dressed, he's one of those pitchers who generates his power from his rear end and thighs, which gives him a bit of a pear shape. The bar is crowded with a few young men and many more young women attending a computer training seminar, and David shakes his head ruefully. "I don't do that anymore," he says, reminding us of his young wife and baby back home in Hickory, North Carolina, "but it's hard with so much prime beef around." After a few minutes, I played an interviewer's trick and asked him a question to which I knew the answer. During BP one day, he'd told me his theory of hitters, and I wanted to get Darrell's reaction.

"There are three kinds of hitters," Lundy obliged. "Just three. In fact, if you watch guys take their swings in the on-deck circle, they will tell you what they are. Most are either divers or spinners. Divers lean out and look for the outside pitch to hit it the other way. Spinners turn on the ball and drive it. Once you figure this out, pitching gets a little easier. Divers like the ball away, so you pitch them inside. Spinners want to pull the ball, so them, you throw away.

"You"—Lundquist turned and looked straight at Darrell—"I've watched you swing." He took a pull at his drink. "Classic spinner." The old slugger laughed. "I'd throw you away all day," Lundy added.

"You keep it out there and you'd probably get me, too." Darrell was still smiling, and staring straight back. "But it's not so easy to keep it on the black all day, and you know you don't want to make a mistake." It was Lundy's turn to smile and stare. They were sitting two stools apart, but it might as well have been sixty feet six inches. Finesse, deception and subtlety have their place in the game, but not between these two. There was mutual respect in the smiles and the tone of voice, and an edge in their eyes.

"You said three types of hitters," I prodded.

"Divers and spinners, like I said, and then there are balanced hitters."

"Where do you pitch them?" Darrell asked.

"Well, now, that's a problem," Lundquist replied. "Them you have to pitch to."

When I asked Lundy why he was in independent ball, he pointed to his right shoulder. "I'm what they call a max-effort pitcher," he said. "I don't have that nice, smooth motion. When I throw, you can hear me grunt on every pitch. Over time, the capsule was damaged and my shoulder would pop out." He twitched at the memory. "You can't believe how much that hurts. The first operation, they could only repair some of the damage. August '95. A month later they went back in and repositioned the capsule, they moved it forward. Look"—he sat up straight and square—"you can see that my right shoulder is different, it's in front of the other one." Noticeably forward, now that I looked, and maybe a little lower, too.

"I had to have the operation to get rid of the pain and they told me I was done with big-time baseball. The advice was to go back to school. I went through rehab, and after two years, I could only throw 85–86. When you don't throw as hard as you used to, you have to find another way to get hitters out, you have to learn to fool 'em. Before the operation I threw hard, but when I came back, I learned a little more about pitching. I worked and worked, and by spring training last year, I topped out at 97. Dr. James Andrews, the guy who did the operation, he said he couldn't understand it, he said I shouldn't be able to play."

In the spring of 1999, Lundy was in the White Sox training camp in Tucson, Arizona. "Jerry Manuel, the manager, he said the same thing that a lot of managers say in spring training, you know, 'If you have any questions, my door is always open.' Well, nobody ever asks, but I did. I'd done well, so I went in and said, I think I deserve to make the team, and I asked him, Where do I stand? He said, 'You've impressed us, but you know, there are only so many places on the team. It's sad, but we can only take eleven pitchers north. You've done well, but . . .' And this is where I expected a ticket back to Triple A, but he said, 'We have to take you with us. You're one of the eleven.' He didn't even crack a smile. It was really neat. My parents were there, they hadn't seen me pitch since '95, but they were there in the stands in Tucson that day."

He did not tell Jerry Manuel that his shoulder was hurting again. "Would you? I knew I wasn't right, but I'd earned my shot and I wasn't going to give it up. I'm a guy who spent six years in A ball. Seven in the minors overall. It's an honor to make it to the very top of the profession you chose when you were five years old, and I wasn't going to give that up for anything. I played in the major leagues, and that's quite an accomplishment."

The pain did not go away, and he pitched poorly. By June he was back in the minors and by September, back on the operating table. After the surgery, the White Sox released him. "Teams told me they want to see me throw 93–95 with some consistency, throw hard and dominate." He needed a place to pitch. A year after pitching in Comiskey Park, David

Lundquist walked onto a community college ballfield to try out for the Aberdeen Arsenal.

"It was hard to come here, and that's not about pride. I don't consider this a comedown. There are a lot of guys in this league with more time in the majors than me. But my agent explained that if I want to get back, this was my only option. I'd never heard of the Atlantic League, I asked if it was Double A. He said it was independent, and I said, 'Oh, shit.' I didn't know what this league was all about, I thought it was like the Northern League, where they have girls pitching. I didn't know what to expect."

He certainly didn't expect to get hammered.

In 14 innings over eight appearances for Aberdeen, he allowed 20 earned runs. The last of them came on a mammoth home run by Hector Villanueva high and far over the left-field fence in Atlantic City. Hector was one of the Atlantic League players with more major league time than Lundquist. At one time, he was Greg Maddux's personal catcher on the Chicago Cubs, but that was many beers ago. These days, Hector looked more like a sumo wrestler than a ballplayer and after giving up that homer, Lundquist decided to quit, and drove home.

"I planned to stay with my family and, you know, maybe go back to school or—well, the fact is that I hadn't thought that far into it, but baseball was a dead end for me. Three surgeries is a lot for a shoulder to take. Enough is enough."

His decision was final for a week. "I'd wake up and wonder what time the bus is, and then I realized that I had no ballfield to go to. It was a major shock, I couldn't figure out what to do during the day." Fearing the worst, he went to see his surgeon, who told him there was no new injury. "He gave me a cortisone shot, and basically, he told me to stop being a baby and get out there and let it go. And you know, it's still in me. The travel sucks, the money sucks, there are a lot of variables, but it came down to the fact that I didn't want to hang it up."

He threw better when he returned, and he came to a new appreciation of Hector Villanueva. He faced the big man three more times. In Atlantic City in mid-August, he got Hector down in the count, one ball and two strikes, and tried to beat him with a fastball inside. Hector ripped it over the left-field fence for three runs. A week later the Surf made their one and only visit to Thomas Run Park, and Hector got him again, a solo homer this time, a majestic, towering shot to left. The fences at Thomas Run were notoriously short, but, as the old joke has it, this one would have gone out at Yellowstone Park. Two days later, in the last game of the year between the two teams, Lundy worked the count to 2 and 2, Hector took a huge cut at a fastball outside and missed.

"That," Lundquist said emphatically, "was the highlight of my season. Remember what I told you about the three different types of hitters? Well, this guy Hector can be all three at different times. I've never seen anybody make those adjustments, move his feet and his stance and his swing the way he does. Talk about balance! Getting him out was a major event. I'd love to face him every day. That's what I mean about competition, that's what drives me out there. I love to battle. You know, the batter's up there, and he's trying to get you out of the game, and that's what I love, because sometimes they can't touch me."

Some call this the Last Chance League, and for players like David Lundquist, the Atlantic League provided an opportunity to play his way into shape after surgery and find out if the velocity and the desire were still there.

Tom Wright is still looking for his first chance.

I met Tom Wright at the batting cage at Thomas Run in mid-June. The Lehigh Valley Black Diamonds were in town with a couple of new players. Manager Wayne Krenchicki, who doubled as Lehigh Valley's GM, told me that one guy had just been released from the Braves Double A team: switch-hitter, not a lot of pop, good glove.

And what about Tom Wright?

"Him?" He thought for a minute. "You know, to be honest, I don't know where we picked him up."

Wright was just finishing up his turn in BP, so I stopped to introduce myself on the way back to the press box, and asked a few of the basic questions.

"Where did you play last year?" A brief stint with the Adirondack Lumberjacks. "Where are you from?" Utah, Salt Lake City. "And how old are you?" Forty-one.

I said thanks and turned to hurry back to the press box when I did the take.

"Forty-one?"

Wright nodded, smiled and touched his fingers to the gray beginning to fringe his brown hair. "I come by this honestly."

A little Grecian Formula, and he could have passed for thirty. Tom Wright is in fabulous condition, a handsome man whose sharp blue eyes and regular features suggest Tom Cruise. I didn't have time to do more than wish him good luck, one fogey to another.

Wright was the designated hitter in the Black Diamonds lineup that day and the next. He got eight chances at the plate, made no hits and struck out five times.

It was no surprise to learn that he'd been cut.

I next saw Tom wearing spikes, baseball pants and a T-shirt, sitting alone in the Surf dugout as the Arsenal arrived at the Sandcastle in Atlantic City a week or two later. As I walked over, the rain that had been threatening for some time started to fall in buckets and Tom told me that it had just washed out a scheduled tryout. He said he had a copy of his résumé and a videotape out in his truck if I wanted to see them. Sure. We walked under the stands, through the clubhouse and out to the parking lot, where he rummaged through one of the six big garbage bags in the back of a road-weary red Toyota pickup truck with Utah plates.

"I've been staying with people from my church and in motels, but I don't have anyplace else to keep my stuff." He handed me a videotape and a professionally printed piece of tan paper and carefully retied the corners of the black plastic bag. Rainwater drained from the corner of the truck bed and ran down his leg. "It hasn't been easy, this last year especially, but I just have to hope somebody will give me my shot."

Since the rain gave both of us a little time, I invited Tom to join me up in the visitors' radio booth. He told me to go ahead and get out of the rain while he changed out of his spikes. When I got upstairs, I had a moment to look at Tom's résumé, and my jaw dropped again.

> OBJECTIVE: To Hit Over .300 With 40–60+
> Home Runs In A Major League Season
> Playing In The Outfield

That's not unreasonable for Barry Bonds or Ken Griffey, Junior, maybe, but as I scanned down the page, it became clear that Tom Wright had never played a full season of professional baseball at any level. When he arrived in the booth and sat down, Tom confirmed that he did not have a lot of game experience.

"In the regular season, counting the three with the Black Diamonds," he said, "I guess I've played in seven or eight games."

"This year?"

"Total."

Tom explained that he'd played baseball in high school in California, and very well, too, but had competed as a swimmer in college. He got the call to baseball after graduation, while he was on the two-year religious mission for the Church of Jesus Christ of Latter-day Saints, the Mormons.

"I feel like one reason we're put here on earth is to develop our talents. When I was on my mission, I evaluated my skills, my abilities, and realized that baseball is my greatest talent. I wanted to spend the rest of my life doing what I do best. I was twenty-seven years old when I got back from my mission, twenty-seven and a half, and baseball has been the focus of my life since then, what I've wanted to do for my career."

Except no one will let him play.

He first tried a couple of junior colleges in Utah. "When I asked why I was being cut, the only explanation I received was 'You're closer to my age than that of the players.'"

The next stop was professional ball, which he quickly learned is not set up to develop late bloomers.

"Age is baseball's way of winnowing people out of the game. There are other factors, too, but age is a big part of it. If you're this many years old and you didn't reach such-and-such a level, they don't care what you can do."

By and large, this is true. Kids start up the minor league ladder at seventeen or eighteen and move up as a group. Until they get to Double A or Triple A, they don't meet a lot of older players. By the time someone's twenty-seven, organized base-

188 • NEAL CONAN

ball figures if they're not in the major leagues, or close to it, they're probably not going to make it. The Atlantic League is full of twenty-seven- and twenty-eight-year-olds in that category, guys who spent years working their way through the minor league ladder. It's conceivable that one or two may show enough to make the scouts reconsider, but Tom Wright started ten years late.

"My friends said, You'll never do it. You're trying to buck the system, and the system is set up a certain way. But if we all thought that way, we'd all end up just following each other. We need to follow our dreams, and I had the ability to run and hit and throw with just about anybody out there, so that's what I focused on in hopes that somebody would give me the opportunity to prove myself."

Over the next fourteen years, Tom Wright attended dozens of tryout camps, with, for example, seven different teams in the Mexican League. In 1995, the strike year when major league teams were looking for replacement players, he was in camp with the Yankees. Last year he tried out for a team in the independent Northern League. "I hit .358 with a home run and three stolen bases in 17 at-bats, and they put me on waivers. When I asked why, the only thing they said was 'It's our decision.' People tell me they don't care about how old I am, but then they release me for no good reason!"

Without real competition, Tom Wright's experience consists of thousands of afternoons, alone, throwing baseballs at a wall and taking swings against a pitching machine. He has a degree in physical education from Brigham Young University and makes his living as a personal trainer. This season, as he realized that time was running out, he made a videotape to showcase his skills.

John Fogerty's anthem "Center Field" plays over images of Tom Wright as he works his way through a series of exercises, lifts and sprints: Tom Wright throwing a baseball, Tom Wright swinging a bat and, in a final astonishing sequence, Tom Wright leaping to the top of a big box that looks to be at least three feet off the floor.

In an interview conducted by a friend, Tom explains why he started baseball late, about his tryouts and his frustrations. Why not lie about your age? "I thought about it, but it's not the right thing to do. I'm a Mormon, for one thing, and I've received advice from former major leaguers like Dale Murphy, Vernon and Vance Law, to be honest. Well, I did, and it's kept me out of baseball."

The video impressed Joe Klein, the executive director of the Atlantic League, who invited Tom to the league's spring training camp. An injury kept Tom from playing there, but Klein kept his name on file, and when Lehigh Valley found itself scuffling for ballplayers, Tom Wright got a phone call.

"I was in Salt Lake, so I had to drive fifteen hundred miles. I got there, and the manager wanted me to play that night. I asked for a little time, so he put me in as the DH the next day." This was the day before the Black Diamonds arrived at Thomas Run to play the Arsenal, and Wright had no luck in his first game, either. "I felt I was just jumping at the ball, I was too eager. I hadn't seen live pitching in so long, my timing was off."

Afterward, I asked Lehigh Valley manager Wayne Krenchicki why he'd decided to release Wright so quickly, and he said he hadn't shown very much. I cross-checked with Darrell, who just shook his head. Alex Andreopoulos, who'd been behind the plate catching when Wright was hitting, happened to be sitting there and said, "Too slow. He couldn't get around on the fastball and we never had to throw him anything else."

The tryout with Atlantic City didn't work out, so Tom Wright drove on to Newark. "I hit a ball farther than anyone I saw hit—and I was watching—in four days of batting practice. Yes, farther than Ozzie Canseco! Am I the only one who sees these things?"

In the course of a long conversation, I tried to suggest several times that maybe his goals were unrealistic, but Tom refused to entertain doubts. "Why? Because God is with me. He has strengthened me and blessed me with a great talent and ability. I can play in the major leagues and put up significant numbers there, yes, even at my age, because God is with me!"

After a moment, I said, "You love baseball, but clearly, it's not loving you back."

Another moment.

"No, it isn't." Tom took a deep breath. "It's been very cruel to me. I've been through a lot of heartache and I've put my family through a lot of heartache. It's just very hard for me to go to my grave thinking, I could have done it, and if I don't get the chance, it's hard for me even to be near a baseball field because it just causes pain. Every time I see a game on TV, I think, That could have been me, I could have done that. And it's hard for me to live with that.

"I don't need more than thirty or forty at-bats, I'm not asking for the world. I've invested fourteen years of my life here, and I just want thirty or forty at-bats to see what I can do."

On March 5, 2001, Tom Wright copied me on an e-mail he was sending out:

> You might know me or have heard my story. I'm writing to you about playing for your team during the upcoming 2001 season.
>
> I am a knuckleball pitcher. I can throw it consistently for strikes with a LOT of movement. I also have a fastball (mid-80s), change-up and slider.
>
> I have traveled all over the U.S. and Mexico trying to get the opportunity to show everyone what I can do. Because of my age, it has been very difficult. For this reason, I have focused on the knuckleball, since age is not that big of a deal and because I have the talent to throw it.
>
> Please let me know if you're interested in having me try out or play for your team during the upcoming season.

10

ATLANTIC LEAGUE STANDINGS						
THROUGH GAMES OF AUGUST 4						
NORTH DIVISION	**W**	**L**	**PCT.**	**GB**	**STREAK**	**LAST 10**
Bridgeport	12	8	.600	—	L 1	7–3
Newark	10	9	.526	1.5	W 1	9–1
Nashua*	10	9	.526	1.5	L 1	3–7
Long Island	11	10	.524	1.5	W 1	4–6
SOUTH DIVISION						
Atlantic City	11	6	.647	—	W 3	7–3
Aberdeen	8	11	.421	4.0	W 1	4–6
Lehigh Valley	7	11	.389	4.5	L 5	3–7
Somerset*	8	13	.381	5.0	L 1	3–7

*Won first half.

I knew we were in trouble when Grumpy left.

The rudimentary facilities at Thomas Run Park restricted the concessionaires to the most basic baseball food groups: peanuts, pretzels and hot dogs, which came in two sizes, "heartburn" and "angina." Kitchens at modern ballparks turn handsome profits on everything from sushi to crab cakes and at the beginning of the season, Grumpy's Barbecue occupied the high end of the Arsenal food chain.

At the start of every home stand, pickup trucks hauled a squat black smoker and a small retail trailer up to a spot behind the press box on the first-base side. The powerful aroma from the smoker was irresistible. The couple who ran the place—I knew them only as Mr. and Mrs. Grumpy—told me that a ballgame didn't last long enough to smoke anything properly. The savory smells that wafted through the ballpark were strictly for advertising, but the steak delivered on the promise of the sizzle. Grumpy's served a very nice pulled pork sandwich and the smoked turkey was good, too. The pit beef was fabulous, thin, tender medium-rare slices stacked high on a kaiser roll. Add a couple of spoonfuls of horseradish and a big squirt of barbecue sauce, and stand back!

While the press box crew were devoted customers, Mr. and Mrs. Grumpy were losing money. I knew that they hadn't renewed their contract, but it was still a shock to come into Thomas Run Park in early August and find their spot empty. A bit farther up the first-base side, two-thirds of the rented Porta Potties were gone, too. The signal was as unmistakable as a white flag fluttering from the pole in center field.

Doubt about the future of the team contributed to the anemic attendance. One of my standard pitches on the radio broadcasts was that after Ripken Stadium opened next season, fans would want to be able to tell stories about the old days at Thomas Run and say they were there when. This might have been more effective if they could see that construction was under way and watch the work proceed. The groundbreaking ceremony at the site off I-95, tentatively scheduled for May first, was pushed back, a month the first time, and then indefinitely. Even the rumors got postponed; the ownership would meet to decide the team's fate just after the Fourth of July, then sometime in mid-August, then Labor Day, for sure.

Everything hinged on contracts for the skyboxes at Ripken Stadium. GM Keith Lupton and managing owner Peter Kirk, veterans of three successful minor league launches in Maryland, said they'd never encountered such stiff sales resistance from the local business community. They fired a couple of salesmen, one of whom told me bitterly that the problem was the cost and the length of the contracts the Arsenal demanded. "Nobody I talk to is willing to make a ten-year commitment," he said, "not even in this economy." Gary Helton, who marketed underwriting announcements for the radio broadcasts to some of the same companies, said that advertising directors told him they'd be laughed out of the boardroom if they recommended the proposals the Arsenal were offering.

But those local businesses didn't bite on the much shorter and vastly cheaper opportunity to sponsor the broadcasts, either. When he sold the baseball project to his boss at Harford Community College, Gary was told that his job was riding on it. Success was not strictly defined in monetary terms. If carrying the Arsenal generated a little publicity and a little goodwill, breaking even would probably be okay. Since I was paid by the team, the only costs to the station were a couple of thousand dollars for equipment and long-distance charges for the telephone line used to feed the audio.

We got one sponsor all season, a local dot-com that bought a month's worth of announcements for $500, which had to be split with the team.

Would-be sponsors argued persuasively that the only way they had to estimate the size of the radio audience was by the tiny numbers that attended home games. The local newspaper, the *Aegis*, excoriated its own readers for failing to support the team: "Attendance," the *Aegis* editorialized in midseason, "frankly has been pathetic. For those who attribute this show of disinterest to the games being played in a community field for amateur teams, albeit a nice one, we say that's a lame excuse."

The lamest excuse I heard was that some in the area resented the team's identification with the city of Aberdeen. Folks from tony communities like Fallston and Bel Air apparently saw no reason to associate with anything named for the small piece of the South Bronx on the wrong side of the interstate. The magic of the Ripken name and word of mouth about the minor league experience were supposed to overcome such obstacles, but people still stayed away in droves.

One outside observer, Tom King of the *Nashua Telegraph*, attributed the Arsenal's attendance problem to several factors: "ridiculous" admission prices ($8 for general admission and $12 for a "box" seat), the failure to get a beer license and a basic lack of publicity. "Not on [the team's] part, because the media relations people know the job, but it's simply tough when there isn't a suburban daily paper to cover the club." The *Aegis*, which is based in Bel Air, published twice a week. "The *Baltimore Sun* is the only daily newspaper," King noted, "and it runs a minor league notebook in its Monday editions which nets the Arsenal about a paragraph's worth of publicity. It's a vicious cycle."

To be fair, the *Sun* didn't cover any of the other minor league teams in Maryland any better, but unlike Bowie, Frederick, Salisbury and Hagerstown, Aberdeen and Harford County were part of the *Sun*'s core market. When the big daily newspaper didn't take the local team seriously, nobody else did, either.

A winning ball club would not have answered all of the problems, but it would have helped. The schedule at the start of the second half was rough—16 of the first 19 games were away. If the Arsenal could stay reasonably close, though, they had a great shot. The last three weeks of August, they had lots of home games, most of them against the weak teams in the South. For some reason, the schedule pitted them against the tougher North Division in September. As I looked ahead, I figured that they needed to be in first place or very close to it when they squared off against the Patriots in Somerset over the Labor Day weekend to have any realistic chance.

It didn't begin well. In the first game of the second half, the Bluefish strafed Zac Stark for 7 runs in the first four innings and went on to win 12–0. Zac, who'd started the season so well, was probably the biggest disappointment of the year. From 5–1, he lost three games in a row, the last an ugly blowout in Atlantic City where he gave up 13 runs in an inning and a third. Next time out, he finally won his sixth game, and then went into free fall. His confidence and command were gone. Earlier, he always seemed to be ahead on the count, and he got hitters to smack his sinkers and sliders on the ground where not even Arsenal infielders could miss them all. These days, the tall lefty slouched out to the mound miserably, his shoulders slumped, his eyes down, beaten before he threw the first pitch. Now, the counts were always in the batter's favor, the sinkers stayed up and the sliders hung. He was so deep in the manager's doghouse that I found him positioned beyond the left-field fence in batting practice, fetching home-run balls. "I don't know what it is," he said disconsolately. "A combination of bad luck and bad pitching." He started to lay some of the blame on his infield, which deserved it, but pulled back. "I won with them before, so I have to figure it's me. I don't know. I just don't know."

The carnage continued the next day as the Bluefish romped, 10–1. We took the Port Jeff ferry across the sound to Long Island, but the team still seemed shellshocked and promptly fell behind against the Ducks. Bud Harrelson had transformed the other expansion team to reflect his style; the Ducks stressed team speed, defense and pitching. Their bullpen was the best in the league and it was very tough to overtake them late in the game. In the seventh inning, though, Danny Perez hit a long homer to get the Arsenal close and the unlikely combination of Matt Taylor and Jose Cepeda triggered a game-winning rally in the eighth. "That," Darrell said afterward, "was really key. You hope you look back at the end of the season and say that was the start of something. We got three two-out hits in a row, and that's one of those things that means so much in the clubhouse. Momentum means so much in the game of baseball, and it's those key plays that pick everybody up."

The dramatic win did seem to steady the club. They drubbed the Ducks 13–3 the next day, did well enough in a home-and-home series against Nashua to survive a sweep in Newark and split a four-game set in Bridgeport. They came home in mid-August with a record of 8–11, not what they'd hoped for, but in second place just four games behind Atlantic City. In their first series at home, they took two out of three from the hapless Lehigh Valley Black Diamonds and looked set to make their run.

Somerset came in next, and a key moment came in the first inning in the next game. Andy Bair was the starter for Aberdeen, a big, goofy-looking local kid who'd given up baseball after three injury-plagued seasons in the low minors. Andy worked as a welder and started throwing again when he was offered the opportunity to teach kids to pitch at a local instructional camp. On a whim, he decided to attend an open tryout the Arsenal staged at Thomas Run Park back on April Fool's Day and threw hard enough to earn a contract. At first, he was all over the place. He lost his first three decisions and then, in Newark one day, it was as if you could see the light go on over his head. He learned to trust his good fastball, got ahead of the hitters and forced them to chase pitches out of the strike zone. His elbow flared up his next time out, though, and now, after a stint on the disabled list, he seemed to be rounding into form just when the Arsenal needed him most.

The second Patriot batter of the game belted a wicked shot that took one hop and kangarooed into Andy's crotch. He wasn't wearing a protective cup and the big lefty fell over as if he'd been shot and crawled toward the third-base line in agony. Many in the crowd that night were family and friends and the ballpark fell silent as he was carted away in an ambulance.

His worried teammates played the next few innings in a fog. Somerset blitzed them for 13 runs on 16 hits and 5 Arsenal errors, several of the unforgivable variety. To everyone's enormous relief, Andy returned to the ballpark late in the game, walking very awkwardly but still among the living. A suddenly energized team put together one of the great rallies of the season, pushing ten runs across the plate on ten hits in the eighth inning, but it wasn't enough.

Darrell was furious. The fact that a guy got hurt was no reason to lose focus and give away a ball game. Ten-run innings are supposed to be enough to win. A lot of the players couldn't understand his anger and thought he was callous. Whatever the reason, the life drained out of the team. Somerset swept them in their own ballpark. A listless Arsenal club went up to Atlantic City and got hammered again. Luckily, a monsoon swept through South Jersey and washed out the last two games in AC. Because that was Aberdeen's last scheduled visit to the Sandcastle, those two rainouts were shifted to Thomas Run Park, but I didn't think it would make any difference.

Before the first-place Surf arrived for what would now be a five-game set, the Arsenal had a chance to get well against the Black Diamonds. As difficult as Aberdeen's circumstances were, Lehigh Valley had it much tougher. A founding chapter of the Atlantic League, the Black Diamonds played their first season, 1998, in Newburgh, New York, while they awaited construction of their ballpark near Easton, Pennsylvania. The stadium wasn't ready for the beginning of the following year, so Lehigh Valley played the entire first half of the year on the road. Then it got worse. Owner/developer Tom Flaherty ran out of money, construction stopped and the future of the team shifted from the suddenly silent stadium site to the courtroom. Flaherty sued the Atlantic League, among others, and operated his team on a shoestring while fighting off bankruptcy. With no home field at all, the Black Diamonds finished out the year on the road.

"It was really hard," said manager Wayne Krenchicki. "A lot of people don't understand the things we had to go through last year. Every third day you were packing up your stuff and putting it back on the bus and traveling after the game. We hung in there as well as I could have dreamed. Late in the season, we were only four games out, but we ran out of gas. Our pitchers still threw pretty well, but the bats started to get heavier, and we went right down the tubes."

A lot of people in the Atlantic League thought that Krenchicki deserved to be named Manager of the Year for holding the Black Diamonds together in 1999. This season he was up for sainthood. With Flaherty still in court and the ballpark still half finished, Lehigh Valley played its home games at an American Legion field in Quakertown, Pennsylvania, a facility that made Thomas Run Park look like Camden Yards.

"I knew coming into this season that it was going to involve a lot more than just running a baseball club between the lines," Krenchicki said. "Me and my pitching coach [Steve Foucault] have tried to do the best we could. The circumstances have been very tough, it's something that hurts quite a bit, but we go on one day at a time and try to put the best ball team we can out there." Sometimes the players' paychecks arrived late and sometimes, they bounced. When the team arrived in Quakertown, there were no ties to that community, no host families to house ballplayers, and local landlords, well aware of the team's financial difficulties, demanded money up front for six-month leases. Pitcher Marshall Boze, an outdoorsman who grew up in Alaska, proposed to set up camp and live in a nearby state park. Krenchicki said, "The first time I heard that, I asked him, 'Are you crazy?,' but they went out and bought tents, there was about four of 'em it started with, and sleeping bags. I went out there a couple of days later, after they were out there, and it was absolutely gorgeous. Now we've got, I think eleven players, my pitching coach and his wife and our trainer all camping out."

As beautiful as the site might have been, it didn't make baseball any easier. "When half your team wakes up in sleeping bags at a campground and they pick up laundry and change in a men's room and go play a game and change again in a men's room and go back to a campground, it's awfully tough over the course of a season."

On August 15, the Black Diamonds were at the hotel in

Aberdeen when their checks failed to arrive yet again, and now the team was late with their meal money, too. Keith Lupton called me into the press box and said the game might have to be canceled because Lehigh Valley's players refused to play.

The phone rang. The league's executive director, Joe Klein, called to say that he was on his way down to Aberdeen to try to resolve the situation and probably wouldn't arrive at the Sheraton until maybe seven. Game time. He asked Keith if he would call the game off on account of the weather. Keith glanced out at the clear blue sky, shook his head and said no. With fans beginning to arrive and the start of my pregame show approaching rapidly, we had to say something to explain why the visiting team wasn't there. Keith and Joe finally agreed to announce that the Black Diamonds were delayed because of "transportation difficulties."

When Klein arrived in Aberdeen, he told the angry Black Diamonds that the league would guarantee their salaries, and the crisis was averted. They got to Thomas Run about an hour late. They didn't win that night, but they did take two of the first three and Aberdeen had to scramble to win the finale.

The disappointing split with Lehigh Valley dropped Aberdeen into third place, just half a game in front of the Black Diamonds and six full games behind Atlantic City. Because of the earlier rainouts, they had five games with the Surf in three days and needed to win at least four to have any hope of hanging in the race.

Game One: In the first game of a doubleheader, Jose Cepeda went 4 for 4 to lead a 17-hit attack and the Arsenal cruised, 15–3.

Game Two: Liam Healy led the Aberdeen hit parade this time, smacking three singles. Zac Stark pitched well for the first time in months. The Arsenal won, 13–5, but lost catcher

Alex Andreopoulos, who pulled a hamstring legging out a double.

Game Three: The Arsenal racked up 17 more hits—that made it 45 in the three games—and blew the Surf away again, 12–3. This was getting interesting.

Game Four: This one was a nail-biter. The Arsenal scored two in the sixth to pull ahead, the Surf rallied back to tie it, then, in extra innings, Aberdeen put two men on base with no outs and watched Atlantic City's pitcher panic after he fumbled a sacrifice bunt. His throw sailed wildly down the right-field line and Gil Martinez raced home with the winning run.

Game Five: The Surf went ahead for the first time in the series when they scored a run in the top of the first inning, but the Arsenal came back with five in the bottom half of the first, plated two more in the second and then two more in the third. Aberdeen won again, 13–8, but lost another key player to a hamstring injury, Gil Martinez this time.

When the smoke cleared, Atlantic City clung to a one-game lead over both Aberdeen and Somerset, but the AC pitching staff had just been eviscerated and would not recover. The Surf was dead. After watching the Arsenal suffer so many difficult losses, it was sweet to see the guys whoop it up, laughing and clapping each other on the back as they took the celebration out to the locker room.

The Dyno-Mite Lady arrived an hour and a half before game time in the middle game of the Atlantic City series, plenty of time to choreograph her self-detonation and give a pregame interview besides. Alison Bly is a full-figured woman of a certain age whose assets are barely contained by a tightly tugged shirt tied at the midriff and a pair of denim cutoffs trimmed in lace. It is a steamy summer afternoon and she's brought her own thunder. She sashays over to the bleachers behind home plate in sandals with five-inch lifts, a performance that draws the immediate attention of Atlantic City Surf manager Tommy Helms, who comes over to the backstop as I start to set up the tape recorder.

"Let me interview her, willya?"

Tommy Helms was Rookie of the Year in the National League in 1966. He's added glasses, gray hair and a few pounds around the middle since then, but, as he leaned up against the chain-link fencing behind home plate, it was clear he'd never lost his boyish leer.

"Where you from, honey?"

Originally, she says, North Carolina. It turns out that manager Helms is a Tarheel, too, and he ladles on some extra drawl.

"Do you like grits?"

"I love grits."

"I do, too." She crosses her legs and picks up the conversation.

"How long?" She smiles. "How long does it take to cook 'em?"

"Grits?"

"Umm-hmm."

Tommy's face twists in concentration.

"To make real ones, you gotta cook 'em like rice."

"Right!"

His bona fides established, Helms warms to the subject.

"You gotta put alotta butter and alotta salt and pepper on 'em."

"Umm, yumm."

"And maybe"—I swear he winked—"maybe a little red-eye gravy on 'em, too."

"Oh, that sounds good. You must like that cholesterol."

"Umm-hmm."

She flips back her short blond do.

"Live hard, die young, and leave a beautiful corpse," she laughs. "My motto."

Wonderfully apt for a woman who makes her living blowing herself up.

Alison Bly represents a peculiar form of American entertainment that works between innings of minor league baseball games. The classic promotional attraction at ballgames was Max Patkin, the late Clown Prince of Baseball. Wearing a hopelessly baggy uniform, his cap askew over a well-traveled and expressive schnozz, Patkin specialized in broad send-ups of the ballplayers' familiar routines. He would elaborate a pitcher's windup into a corkscrew, ape a third-base coach's signs, and isolate each of a batter's gestures—the scratch, the shrug, the tap on the spikes—before coiling himself into a pretzel and peering ferociously out at the mound, all of this in a Buster Keaton deadpan.

Nobody wants to admit it, but Max Patkin was a mime. He didn't wear a striped shirt and white face, but Marcel Marceau would have envied the way he defined the space of the batter's box. The silent act adapted well to baseball, too. Public address systems evolved slowly and a lot of ballparks around the minors still have trouble getting a field microphone to work for the national anthem.

But even the baseball clowns work with music these days, cassette tapes delivered to the public address announcer, along with a briefing and a script. Myron Noodleman, for example, is a one-man act subtitled The Dancing Nerd. This is a character with short black hair, big glasses, bow tie, shirt cuffs shooting out of plaid jacket sleeves that end halfway between the wrist and elbow and pants six inches too short. There's a bit of Michael Jackson in the choreography, but everything else is Jerry Lewis, circa 1958. Noodleman does this act in front of crowds where the parents are too young to remember "Hey, lady," but they and their kids eat it up. And they say this goes over only in France.

The Chicken is a mime in a bird suit. Mascots never talk, and, for all his subsequent success, The Chicken originated as The San Diego Chicken; his moniker since leaving the Padres has been the subject of legal proceedings. Either good fortune or good planning provided him with a relatively small, light outfit. Aside from the big yellow head, there's not an awful lot of padding, which means a lot on a hot day—believe me, you never want to be in the same room when Splash or Sparky starts taking the suit off.

My personal favorite is an animal act, a dog-and-Frisbee routine called Sky Dogg and Ray. For the big finish, Ray somehow manages to flip two Frisbees, and bends over as two dogs jump up onto and then high off his back, the last landing trustfully in his arms.

Acts that need a more sophisticated sound system have to bring their own. When they visited Thomas Run Park, The Blues Brothers installed a mixing console and a computer between the scoreboard operator and the official scorer and spent a good couple of hours testing to see just how loud they could crank it up. In the middle of the second inning, they made their entrance in the Blues Mobile, a faithful reproduction of the police car from the John Belushi/Dan Aykroyd movie that inspired the routine. "Everybody Needs Somebody to Love" rang out as the car raced in from the right-field corner, nearly catching a little air as it bumped over the mound in the visitors' bullpen. Ersatz versions of Jake and Elwood erupted out of the car near home plate, complete with fedoras, sunglasses and cheap suits.

They used their wireless mikes to shout a few words of encouragement to the fans—"C'mon, everybody, put your hands together"—and then lip-synched a couple of choruses before promising to return later in the game.

All of this in not a lot more than the ninety seconds allotted between innings.

The Blues Brothers Act is five guys and a big RV full of equipment. Food, gas and hotels bring their price to well over three thousand dollars a show. It started as two guys doing a party routine at halftime of a college basketball game, but over the last fifteen years, it's developed into one of the biggest, best and most profitable acts of its kind. It was discouraging to learn that this road show never bothered to get rights to mimic all this material. It was almost ten years before Dan Aykroyd's attorneys noticed, and, last I heard, negotiations were still under way.

The Dyno-Mite Lady is not original, either. The act started decades ago as Captain Dyno-Mite.

"He was a retired merchant marine, eighty-five years old when I met him," Alison Bly recalls, "rough and tough and meaner than a snake." Southern courtesy then reasserted itself. "But he was really a nice fella. He had to retire after he had his foot amputated." She attributed the gangrene to a lifetime of work with explosives, which, if true, puts her extremities in imminent danger.

"I started with pipe bombs. I really shouldn't promote this too much, but when we were kids, we made pipe bombs until a friend of mine blew his finger off. Then we put the bombs away and went back to the G.I. Joes and the Barbie dolls for a while."

After high school in North Carolina, Alison joined the army and specialized in demolitions. "When I got out there was a recession on, so I decided to blow myself up to pay the mortgage." In Tampa, Florida, she met Captain Dyno-Mite's agent, Jim Lawrence, who was looking for someone to revive the act, "someone who knew how to handle explosives and someone female who could exploit the costume.

"My first time was in Tampa, at the state fairground, I did a demo there. They all thought I was crazy, but my brother was there and he was the one who kept saying, 'Get in there, you'll be fine,' so he was the one who inspired me to get in the box. So, I'm ready to get in, I was looking for him for a last good-bye, and I couldn't find him anywhere. Finally, I saw him hiding over behind the tires, you know, the ones they stack up on the curve of the racetrack, and he's still going, 'Get in, you'll be all right.' But after it blew up, I said, 'That was great, let's do it again,' and that's how my career began."

I ask what she tells people when they asked what she does for a living.

"I usually say I run a day-care center, just so they don't bother me. If I tell them the truth, I know it's going to be a while, they're going to have so many questions."

She describes herself as a stuntwoman, and bristles a bit when the word "carnival" is mentioned.

"I don't do carnivals and fairs, I don't like that kind of travel. I like first-class hotels, I come in, do my thing, and leave. I like the baseball games, monster-truck shows, and I work indoors as well, with basketball and hockey. I think they used to do this kind of thing in the thrill shows years ago, but what I do now is different, I've dressed it up a bit. I mean, you can't just do the act itself, you have to add something to it, your own personality."

"And a little sex appeal?" I ask.

"Oh, thank you so much!" Even though it's radio, I get an appreciative wiggle. "Yes, that always helps. It's the oldest act in the world and it still works, I guess."

The blast itself is literally over in a flash, so the trick is to play on the tension. The buildup begins as "Thus Spake Zarathustra"—the theme from *2001*—thunders over the PA system. The Dyno-Mite Lady enters through a gate in the right-field corner, wearing a two piece gold lamé outfit, white boots, and a red, white and blue Wonder Woman cape that spills out behind as she prances toward the infield. A blue-and-white Styrofoam box waits on top of a piece of plywood just in front of home plate. The Coffin of Death, the announcer explains in ominous tones, containing the equivalent of a full stick of TNT.

"The explosives I use are my own brew," Bly says, and declines to tell me the secret formula. "The key factor is how you place the charges to explode directionally. But"—she adds a little drama—"there is no room for any error whatsoever."

She swirls off her cape and hands it to her assistant, Alexandra, who, the announcer informs us, is a licensed mortician. The Dyno-Mite Lady dons a crash helmet, steps into the box and, with one last brave salute, crawls down inside.

"Ladies and gentlemen, count down with me if you will." The announcer gets everyone in the ballpark to join in. "Ten, nine, eight"—the box doesn't stir—"seven, six, five"—little kids are screaming out the numbers by now—"four, three, two, one!"

There's a slight pause for effect and then a truly surprising bang, followed by an actual gasp.

"Uh-oh, is the Dyno-Mite Lady okay?"

As a puff of white smoke clears, we can see that she is stretched out, facedown, amid Styrofoam debris that's scattered out to the pitcher's mound.

"Will she survive that thunderous explosion that can sometimes knock you out for several seconds?"

She will. After a few more moments to milk the effect, she slowly rises to salute us again.

"She's okay, ladies and gentlemen! Alison Bly, the world-famous, one and only Dyno-Mite Lady! If you'd like to meet the Dyno-Mite Lady and get autographs, we have a concession area with souvenir baseballs for sale. Thank you very much!"

By her count, this was blast number 1,151 for Alison Bly, and she says there will be but two more.

"After fifteen years of dynamite, I'd like to keep at least one brain cell and what little hearing I have left. I was going to complete the rest of the season, but I'm going to stop a little early because I might have some neurological damage. Sometimes, after I'm done working, the whole right side of my face is numb and I hear a whole lot of ringing, so I think it's time to hang up the helmet and retire the boots."

11

ATLANTIC LEAGUE STANDINGS						
THROUGH GAMES OF AUGUST 20						
NORTH DIVISION	**W**	**L**	**PCT.**	**GB**	**STREAK**	**LAST 10**
Bridgeport	22	13	.629	—	W 2	6–4
Long Island	22	15	.595	1.0	W 1	7–3
Nashua*	17	18	.486	5.0	L 1	4–6
Newark	15	20	.429	7.0	L 1	3–7
SOUTH DIVISION						
Atlantic City	17	16	.515	—	L 5	4–6
Aberdeen	17	18	.486	1.0	W 5	7–3
Somerset*	18	19	.486	1.0	W 1	6–4
Lehigh Valley	12	21	.364	5.0	L 2	3–7
*Won first half.						

*T*he excitement of the AC sweep began to ebb even before we boarded the bus for a trip to Long Island the next day. We had to leave Andy Bair at home to get treatment—in effect, he was gone for the year. His loss, plus the strain of two doubleheaders in three days, seriously depleted the pitching staff. Mike Wolff was done for the season, too. Wolffie had a nagging foot problem that he played with for nearly a month until the pain became too much. He stayed with the team, limping around in an air cast in hope that rest would cure what was initially diagnosed as a ligament strain. A third set of X-rays taken during the home stand revealed a stress fracture and he came down to the hotel to say good-bye before he left for home.

Their thighs heavily wrapped, Andro and Gil limped as badly as Wolff. Their loss left the team with only eight position players, so Darrell had no choice but to use a pitcher as the DH.

"Can you frickin' believe that?" he asked incredulously. "One lousy game out of first and I have to hit a pitcher." In fact, he did have another option. He could put his own name on the active roster. He gave this idea some serious thought, but reluctantly inserted reliever Ron Scott, my housemate, into the lineup as the DH, batting ninth. Scotty rolled a single up the middle his first time up, but came up again at the critical moment of the game, bases loaded, two out, and grounded out softly to short. "Shoot," Darrell said, "I thought maybe that's when the guy gets a hit. That's what happens when everything's going perfect." The Arsenal lost, 3–2.

I could tell from the way he took his cuts in BP the next day that Darrell wanted to get in there and hit and I believe he had to be talked out of the idea. The league was already embarrassed that Aberdeen was using pitchers to hit, but that wasn't exactly big news. If a long-retired former major league star picked up a bat, that might well have made the papers and provided ammunition for writers who like to snigger at the independent leagues. "That was a catch-22," Darrell said. "I didn't want to go out there and kinda taint the game. As far as I'm concerned, the guys we have are the guys we'll play and we'll just have to do the best that we can. I thought about it a little bit," he admitted, "but I don't want to end my career striking out three times the last time I ever play."

Reinforcements arrived from an unusual source. Dan DiPace's son, Danny, played the year in Italy, mostly because that gave him a good shot to play in the Olympics. Anybody whose name ended with a vowel was apparently eligible for the Italian national team and the squad the Italians sent to Sydney included a lot of Italian Americans. There were a couple of weeks between the end of the season in Italy and the opening of the Olympic training camp, so Danny took a flight into JFK and brought a friend with him, catcher Chris Madonna.

Before the next game against the Ducks, I went into the visitors' clubhouse at EAB Park to glean a little information about the new additions. Young DiPace and Madonna were stretched out in the trainer's room trying to get a little sleep, while DiPace the elder was on the phone in the manager's office next door, speaking Italian.

"Well," he said when he hung up, "they can play, but they can't use their real names. Sal"—the Italian baseball impresario with whom he'd been speaking—"says it might screw up their eligibility."

"Well, hell," Darrell said with a sigh, "there's no reason to screw up their chance at the Olympics."

"Oh, no," Dan replied, "this has nothing to do with the Olympics, he's talking about some European tour afterwards. To tell you the truth, I don't know what it is and I don't even think they want to go, necessarily, but I promised Sal he wouldn't see those names on the stat sheet."

"Too late." I held up a copy of the brand-new official roster that the Arsenal front office had just faxed to the press box.

"Shit," Dan said. "Shit, shit, shit." Then, after a second, he asked, "Can you stop those?"

The Ducks stacked rosters, stat sheets and press releases on a table in the press box. With an hour to game time, only one or two copies had been picked up. The critical person, the official scorer, hadn't arrived yet. "Probably."

"You go collect all of those, I'll call Aberdeen and get them to send up a new roster with different names."

"So," Darrell asked, "what do we call 'em?"

"Madonna! Hey, Madonna!" Dan yelled at the sleepy catcher in the next room. "What's your mother's maiden name?"

Which is how Dan Cecile and Chris Cosentino entered the Atlantic League record books.

Both of them got hits—Madonna/Cosentino went 3 for 4—but the Arsenal lost again.

On the bus after the game that night, Chris told me that he grew up on Long Island, but qualified as an Italian citizen because his grandparents had been born in Sicily. "So now me and Danny, we're going to play in the Olympics this year. I'm so excited, I can't wait." Both played for Cus Cantine Ceci Parma, the most northerly of nine teams in a league that stretched down to Nettuno, about an hour south of Rome. "Anybody will tell you that Parma is the best place to live in Italy," he gushed. "The food, the culture, it's a very rich town, in fact the main problem is that it's one of the most expensive places to live anywhere in Italy."

He wouldn't tell me how much he'd been paid, but said, "They treat you right and they really try to make it a good experience for you." In Italy, they only play weekends, a single game Friday night, then doubleheaders Saturday and Sunday. "It's basically the same. Talentwise, it's probably High A,

Double A at best, and there are some different rules, like you have to be an Italian citizen to catch and foreigners can pitch only on Friday night. But the ballparks aren't bad, and since we don't have a lot to do during the week, we take care of our own field. Not the grass, you know, but we're out there fixing the dirt, redoing the mound, that kind of thing. The Italian players work every day, so when they show up at the park, they're really there for the love of the game. It's not a job for them, it's a hobby, so they're out there to play as hard as they can play."

The crowds were the only real disappointment. "There are not a lot of people interested in seeing baseball in Italy, not yet, anyway, so during the regular season, we only get eight hundred, maybe a thousand." I told him he'd feel right at home when we got to Thomas Run.

I also showed him an e-mail that had been faxed up from Aberdeen along with the new rosters. An Italian sportswriter whom Adam Gladstone knew had sent a scouting report.

"Hey, Danny." Chris nudged his teammate in the next seat up. "This guy even knows about Sonia!"

"What?" DiPace stirred. "How'd he know that? What did he say?"

"It just says, 'By the way, when you see DiPace, ask him about Sonia.' Hey, this guy's got you down, listen to this." Madonna laughed. "'DiPace is a good fastball hitter, but changing speeds you can make him struggle, especially pitching to the outside part of the plate.' He's even got your nickname in there, Pacione." He put a lilt into the name: "pu-CHO-nee." He turned to me. "They used to chant that when he came up: 'Pacione, Pacione . . .'"

"So what does he say about you?" DiPace asked, still sleepy.

"'Christopher Madonna is a very experienced catcher.'"

Well, he got that right. 'As a hitter, he was absolutely great for our league. He can call a good ball game, but,'" and his voice began to lose its playful tone, "'he hasn't got a top arm.' Hey, who does this guy think he is, breaking my balls. I threw eight of ten guys out, that's not a top arm? What the hell does he want?"

I reminded him of that "absolutely great hitter" part, but he continued to grumble about the criticism of his throwing. I learned later that Chris had batted over .300 in Double A Trenton one year but was released by the Red Sox after surgery on the elbow in his throwing arm.

Chris and Danny weren't the only Atlantic Leaguers heading for Sydney. Somerset outfielder Glenn Reeves was going home. "It's something I've dreamed of my whole life," the Aussie said. "Representing my country, especially at the Olympics and especially when the games are in my home country, well, it's got to be the greatest achievement in my baseball career so far."

More and more Australians play professionally in the United States, and Reeves explained that the American game became popular down under as a way for cricket players to keep in shape over the winter. "My father was a cricketer and he played baseball for many, many years, and eventually played for the Australian team. I just grew up around the game, and like my dad, I progressed through the levels. I represented my state and I was part of the Australian under-19 team at the Junior Olympics, and played there against a lot of the guys I later played with and against over here, John Roskos and Alex Rodriguez, Preston Wilson, guys like that. Livan Hernandez pitched for Cuba. That's where the Florida Marlins first saw me, and, since Australia's not part of the draft system, they signed me as a free agent."

David Nilsson was the first Australian player to make it big in the United States and he bought the Australian Baseball League, which Reeves describes as semiprofessional still, but coming on strong. "David is very patriotic. Each year, he goes back to Australia and tries to build up baseball and now that he owns the league, he's trying to turn it into something big, a Southeast Asia League, to help develop baseball in Australia." Nilsson, a free agent, turned down offers from major league teams because they wouldn't agree to let him skip the last month of the 2000 season to play for Australia in the Olympics. He signed to play in Japan instead, which didn't work out too well. After a poor start, his team sent him down to the Japanese minors and he ended up going home early. "I think that was great," Reeves said. "He gave up, how many millions of dollars, just to represent Australia in the Olympics in his hometown. He's the glue that'll keep our team together."

Japan's big leagues are far and away the best-paying and most attractive outpost for the American foreign legion. Korea and Taiwan import ballplayers, too, and, though they make good money, some guys have a hard time adjusting to the cultural differences. Tyrone Horne started this season in Korea, and hated it.

"I felt that when I was over there, I felt like it was always about politics. I think Americans get blamed for just about everything. I mean, the team loses, you get blamed for not driving in a run, or not hitting a homer. Being a foreign player, there's twice the pressure; they want you to be perfect."

Korean teams are highly regimented, rising, eating and exercising as one. "The team I was with," said Tyrone, "they eat breakfast, lunch and dinner together every day. Which gets to you after a while. Basically, they served us all Korean food, and I wasn't eating cats and dogs and that stuff, but I got tired of it, you know? I told them I needed some Western food on my own. The food over there, it's too rich for you, really. I think they must all have high blood pressure and heart attacks and stuff 'cause I mean they eat a lot of beef. They had sushi, too, I was eating sushi all the time. It's totally different."

Tyrone said he could have learned to deal with all of that, but the language barrier drove him crazy, and he left after just a couple of months.

"Communications were terrible. Like my situation: I went through four translators and the last one I had, man, he was terrible. He would never translate what they were saying, you know, he made it so polite that I never knew what they were trying to tell me and, basically, I felt that they didn't know what I said, either."

Aaron Jersild, a late-season acquisition who pitched for Somerset and Long Island before coming over to the Arsenal in a trade, played in both Mexico and Taiwan. "Not too long in Mexico," he told me, "just a couple of months, but I spent a whole year in Taiwan. I actually enjoy seeing other parts of the world and it's a lot of fun to meet a lot of new people and play baseball. It was a good experience."

Though Taiwan fielded a long succession of championship Little League teams, professional baseball started there only in 1990. The game quickly became a national obsession and the bookmakers followed the fans. Within a few years, local newspapers reported that gamblers put down more than $1.8 billion over the course of the season, all of it, of course, illegally. You could bet on whether a certain player got a hit or which side of the field the ball would be hit to, and, with the stakes so high, it was only a matter of time before the local mob decided to bet only on sure things.

"Gambling was a huge part of the game over there," Jersild said. "There were always offers to participate in game fixing and all that, it was always there. I actually had it done behind my back when I was pitching a couple of times. There's a core of gamblers on each team that are always in on the fix whenever it's going on, so if you're not agreeing to it, it's going to happen whether you're in on it or not."

It turns out that Taiwanese ballplayers throw games for the same reason the Black Sox fixed the 1919 World Series. The locals are poorly paid and think they're getting screwed by owners whom they see getting rich. In 1997 a Taiwanese media conglomerate paid the Chinese Professional Baseball League $59 million for a two-year TV deal. Foreign players make much better money, but some undoubtedly succumbed to the temptation—Taiwanese players have confessed that they accepted bribes of $145,000 per game. Americans were involved in an incident where gamblers kidnapped five members of the champion Brother Elephants after they lost a game to the lowly Sinon Bulls. Reportedly, mobsters dropped a bundle on the game they thought had been fixed and hired some toughs to teach the players a lesson. Investigations and eventually trials ensued. One U.S. player was indicted but had left the country and was never convicted. The Americans all claimed that they were innocent victims, but why, observers asked, would gamblers bother to rough up players who weren't involved?

As the season went on, it became evident that a lot of the Spanish-speaking players regarded the Atlantic League as an opportunity to make a little money in the summertime and prepare for winter baseball. There are very competitive and, at least by independent standards, well-paying winter leagues in Puerto Rico, the Dominican Republic and Venezuela.

The Arsenal had a frustrating experience with a left-handed pitcher named Alberto Blanco. After a few outings for Aberdeen, Blanco lost the velocity on his fastball and the bite on his curve. Doctors said he had tendinitis and recommended cortisone injections, but Blanco refused; with rest, his arm would be ready for winter ball back home in Venezuela. There, he'd be pitching in front of his relatives and friends and that was where he expected to earn the bulk of his income, too. Understandably, he saw no reason to risk his arm to help Aberdeen, and the Arsenal, understandably, saw no reason to pay him.

The team's ace, Angel Miranda, was chafing to get home to Puerto Rico after an up-and-down season that included a month on the disabled list. As a former major leaguer, he said, "They treat you right in Puerto Rico. This league here, this is bullshit." Accommodations were a constant source of friction with Miranda; he believed he was entitled to a single when he was alone and an extra room when his wife and baby joined him. Sometimes there was confusion about the dates, sometimes extra rooms simply weren't available. Once, Miranda got so angry that he refused to pitch, but changed his mind at the last minute.

To be fair, though, tempers were shortening all around because the team was losing. Despite the efforts of the Italian imports, who played well, the Arsenal won just once on the six-game road trip to fall five games under .500. Luckily, the rest of the South Division was playing badly, too, so Aberdeen was just two games out of first place with the Newark Bears coming into Thomas Run Park for a four-game set before the Labor Day showdown up in Somerset.

Newark was hopelessly out of contention in the North

Division, a last-place team that, for reasons that will always remain mysterious, played like the 1927 Yankees against Aberdeen. In the first game of the year up in The Den, the Arsenal came back from an eight-run deficit to stage one of the most improbable rallies of the season, but after that, the Bears always found a way. Opposite-field pop flies fell in for doubles, weak ground balls found holes in the infield, routine fly balls somehow took wing and sailed over the fence. Ozzie Canseco, who was in the midst of an MVP season for Newark, had nothing to do with it. Ozzie thought Aberdeen had the best pitching staff in the league.

Losing to Newark drove Darrell crazy and with the importance of these games, he called a rare team meeting to reinforce the need for focus and hustle. There was no place to gather inside the field house locker room, so the players assembled on a small set of bleachers next to the tennis courts. I was not invited, but heard the details from several people afterward. Talking about unnecessary distractions, Darrell said he didn't want to see seed-spitting contests or card games or guys reading during the game. Zac Stark, the most avid reader on the club, took this as a personal insult. He stood up slowly, his face turned red. He said, "Have a nice season, Darrell," turned, walked into the locker room, changed into his street clothes and left the team for good.

Darrell was dumbfounded. He had no faith in Zac as a pitcher anymore, but the remark was not intended personally. Several players told me that they didn't take Darrell's remarks as a shot at anyone in particular and thought Zac had overreacted. I suspect that he was so frustrated that he might have been looking for a reason to put an end to what had become a nightmare season. He was pitching so poorly that he was brought into a game only when the team was way behind, so his explosive departure should not have hurt, but the club wasn't the same afterward.

They played a terrible game that night and lost, 13–3. The next day, this message went up on the bulletin board in the locker room:

"Hustle keeps you in the lineup. Only today's relief pitchers and bullpen catchers allowed in the bullpen at any time. NO POUTING ALLOWED. $50 fine automatically taken out of paycheck! No Exceptions!"

They scored six runs in the first inning that night, but lost, 12–7.

At batting practice the next day, Rick Wise called out "Hit and run!" before throwing a pitch to Maleke Fowler. He shortened up his swing and punched a ground ball to the right side, textbook execution. "What are you doing, swinging like that?" barked Darrell from behind the cage. "You can hit a home run on a pitch like that, put a good swing on it!" Maleke's eyes widened, but he knew better than to talk back to his manager on the field and went ahead and took the rest of his cuts. Off to the side of the cage, Asbel Ortiz, normally one of the most enthusiastic players on the team, reacted with disgust.

"Damn! Hit-and-run play, you just put it on the ground and run. I've never had a hitting coach before who wanted you to hit a home run every time up. Garciaparra, Jeter, Edgar Martinez, all those guys are inside-out hitters, and they seem to do all right."

Ortiz, who was in a deep slump, was not in the lineup the next day. During BP, he sat alone on the bench. It was Darrell's turn to react with disgust. "Funny," he said. "You don't see the guys who aren't in the lineup out there taking their ground balls. I guess it's hard to take grounders while you're pouting."

The Bears took three of the four and the Arsenal took the bus up to New Jersey for the crucial Labor Day series against the Patriots needing to win at least two of three to get back into the race. They got blown out in the first game, outpitched in the second and coughed up a late lead to lose the third.

Mathematical elimination was still weeks away, but it was over. The death spiral was excruciating for a while, but the hard words and the hard feelings ebbed away as we played out the string. Once everyone knew they wouldn't win, it became a little easier to look back and realize how long the odds had been from the start.

Even in an independent league, expansion teams start with a handicap. It took time to shake the squad down into a team, and the core that eventually emerged was too small to survive the effects of injury and retirement. The chronic inability to find useful replacements was compounded by the lack of resources to pay them.

Late in the season, for example, Adam Gladstone and Bill Ripken convinced a former major leaguer named Brian Kowitz to try out for the team. Kowitz had once been among the crown jewels of the Atlanta Braves' minor league system and won a World Series Championship with the big club in 1995. The next year, he was traded to the Blue Jays and suffered a severe ankle injury. Mortgage banking proved more attractive than rehab. He was fully recovered and playing a little softball around his home in Pikesville, Maryland, when the Arsenal came calling; he jumped at the chance to play again. Kowitz was a terrific hitter, still, but could only come to home games. There was no way the Arsenal could offer him enough to be a full-time player again.

Being a sentimental old man, I took the collapse of the team's chances harder than the professionals on the field. For them, this was another season and they'd all been part of losing ball clubs before. This was my first team. I told their stories every night, the daily saga of improbable achievement and crushing loss. I was their bard and they were my heroes. I think I fell in love with them a little bit, something that rarely helps your perspective, and I wanted them to win so badly. In the end, I was probably wrong to see the late-season squabbling as more cause than effect. They lost because they didn't have enough good players. They knew that all along and there wasn't enough fairy dust on the planet to change it.

The Italians left after Labor Day and Dan DiPace, Sr., followed a few days later and flew to Australia to watch his son march in the opening ceremony and play in the Olympic Games. The Italian baseball team did pretty well; they beat South Africa, which was expected, and Australia, which wasn't, and they gave Team USA fits in a game that was tied 2–2 until the eighth inning.

The September collapse should not obscure some real achievements. The team was better on Labor Day than it was on Memorial Day. The defense was still poor but not as bad as it was earlier, and the starting pitching was much better.

"I'm proud of the guys," Darrell said. "We had a lot of games on the road and a tough situation here at home. We kept ourselves in the race in both halves and though we didn't play well down the stretch, there were a lot of injuries and other things beyond our control. We lost a lot of close games because we made mistakes and when you play talented teams with more experience, they know how to take advantage of your mistakes.

"You know, experience is such a huge thing. It's a little different situation here than it is for most guys coming out of organizations, you have to go out here and try to win. It's not like you weren't trying to win before, but the urgency wasn't there. That's the number one thing here and in the situation where most of these guys were before, that's not the emphasis. 'As long as I'm getting better, that's the main thing.' Well, that's just not the case here, you have to play hard every day, every at-bat, every pitch. That urgency is more important than they may have realized, and that was a little frustrating at times. It's gotta start the first day of the season. But we played some teams really tough and we beat some teams that didn't think we could beat them. For the most part, we went about it the right way, and that's the main thing."

And there were some personal achievements to celebrate. Gil Martinez battled for the batting title up to the last day of the season and ended up second, with a terrific average of .332. Toward the end, he said he'd probably retire from baseball. Then, with a grin, he told me that he had a softball game in Puerto Rico two days after the Atlantic League shut down.

David Steed had an even better year. At .321, his batting average was fourth best in the league, he finished second in on-base percentage, fifth in slugging and fourth in runs scored. Steeder led the club in homers, hits, runs batted in and runs scored. On the last weekend of the season, his agent called to say that he'd been offered a Triple A contract by the Texas Rangers for 2001.

Ozzie Canseco established league records for home runs and RBIs and was the runaway choice for most valuable player. The Squid, Al Sontag, was voted the Atlantic League's best pitcher. Bud Harrelson was Manager of the Year, small consolation because while his Ducks wound up with the league's best record overall, they finished second to Nashua in the first half, then second to Bridgeport, and failed to make the playoffs.

Due in no small measure to Long Island's spectacular success at the gate, the Atlantic League established a new attendance record.

Having won both halves in the South, the Somerset Patriots stood by and waited for the winner of the playoffs in the North Division. The Bluefish took the first game behind The Squid, but Nashua won the next two to earn a berth in the finals, and then swept the Patriots three straight. According to both Tom King's and Geoff Mosher's accounts, the finale was a classic. The teams swapped haymakers for fourteen innings, the lead changing hands again and again until the Pride finally put the Patriots down for good in the wee hours.

I will not miss the bus. I came to dread the bleary edge of unconsciousness, knowing that if I let myself nod off, my neck would stiffen like concrete. I hated looking forward to the two A.M. stop at the McDonald's outside Bridgeport. "I'll take the unacceptably awful meal, please. And yes, I'm afraid I would like fries with that."

I won't miss midmorning wake-ups, where I have to check the phone book to remind myself what city we're in. And I've dwelled far too long already on the tired metaphor of the hotel-gym treadmill.

And I will not miss losing. This first year, the Arsenal just didn't have the resources of most of the other Atlantic League clubs. They hung in there for a while, but the five-month season tests depth and resilience, qualities that this team exhausted quickly. By the end of the season, they had to struggle to stay out of the cellar. It was uncanny to watch the grim cliché unfold night after night, as the team found another way to lose.

But one of the greatest things about baseball is daily rebirth.

In the warmth of late-summer sunshine, the team reawakened each afternoon amid old jokes and the comfort of pregame rituals. Timelessness and moment intersect in the batting cage. Last night is gone, and there's a new chance tonight. Which is only appropriate in a league composed of kids and castoffs.

I discovered that there's a big difference between a losing season and a lost year. I've learned a lot. Baseball play by play is a study in description and silence and, most important, in narrative. The first two are constant challenges, but narrative is in the structure of the game. We hang on every pitch to hear the answer to the fundamental question of storytelling: and then? AND THEN?

After months of daily installments, it always seemed unfair to me as a listener when my baseball pals just signed off and went away after the last game. It's even worse on the other end. I badly miss being on the radio three hours every day. I miss my daily bicycle race with myself. I made the goal of under an hour, but I know I could've done better. I miss the banter around the batting cage. I miss the guys. And I'd better go now, before I miss the bus.

E P I L O G U E

ATLANTIC LEAGUE FINAL STANDINGS

THROUGH GAMES OF SEPTEMBER 25

NORTH DIVISION	W	L	PCT.	GB	STREAK	LAST 10
Bridgeport	43	26	.623	—	L 1	6–4
Long Island	42	28	.600	1.5	W 1	3–7
Nashua*	38	32	.543	5.5	W 1	6–4
Newark	36	34	.514	7.5	L 1	8–2
SOUTH DIVISION						
Somerset*	36	34	.514	—	L 1	5–5
Atlantic City	32	37	.464	3.5	L 1	5–5
Aberdeen	26	43	.377	9.5	W 1	3–7
Lehigh Valley	25	43	.368	10.0	W 1	4–6

PLAYOFFS

North Division: Nashua defeated Bridgeport, 2 games to 1.

South Division: Somerset advanced with a bye after winning both halves.

CHAMPIONSHIP

Nashua defeated Somerset, 3 games to 0.

*Won first half.

*S*hortly after the end of the season in early October, Charlie Vascellaro called to tell me that the remnants of the Arsenal front office had been loaded into a van and hauled away. The team was dead. I called Darrell at his home in California to commiserate and quickly discovered that this was the first he'd heard of the news.

The end shouldn't have been a surprise. In retrospect, the partners in the enterprise, Peter Kirk and Maryland Baseball and Cal Ripken, Jr., and the Tufton Group, had divergent interests. The Maryland Baseball people wanted to operate the team as a business. Without commitments from local companies on skyboxes and signage, they couldn't finance the loans to start construction or project enough income to support the operation of the team. I believe Peter probably would have gone ahead if the business plan had been anywhere near the break-even point. He wouldn't tell me how much the Arsenal lost in a year, but my best guess is somewhere around one and a half million dollars, at least. Peter and his partners in Maryland Baseball sold their three affiliated franchises, the Delmarva Shorebirds, the Frederick Keys and the Bowie

Baysox, plus a couple of associated baseball-services companies, to a cable television company for a reported $44 million, so 2000 might not have been a bad year to include some serious losses on the tax returns.

The Ripkens remained determined to push ahead with the project on their own. Ultimately, I believe that the family legacy to both baseball and Aberdeen was uppermost in their calculations. After the breakup of the partnership, an amicable divorce from all accounts, the Tufton Group took over the finances and operation of the stadium as well as the baseball academy. They broke ground in the spring of 2001 with a plan to complete Ripken Stadium in time for the 2002 season and to finish the first of the youth fields in time to host the Babe Ruth League championships later that summer. The other fields and the dormitories would follow the year after.

They did not have a team, though. Peter Kirk came out of the divorce with the franchise, the right to operate a team in the Atlantic League. How much that's worth is open to question. The Ripkens, meanwhile, hoped to bring an Orioles affiliate to Aberdeen. In June 2001, Cal Ripken, Jr., announced plans to retire at the end of the season to devote more time to his family and to the baseball academy. That triggered enormous interest in Aberdeen, whetted even further by a story a few days later that the Orioles organization was close to an agreement with its most famous player. Much remained to be worked out, but the plan called for Aberdeen to get a team in the New York–Penn League. That's the lowest level of A ball, with a short, 78-game schedule that runs from mid-June to Labor Day. The minor league teams that the Mets and Yankees moved into New York City, the Brooklyn Cyclones and the Staten Island Yankees, both play in the New York–Penn League.

Over the winter, Tom Flaherty finally exhausted his appeals, and ownership of the Lehigh Valley Black Diamonds reverted to the Atlantic League. If the Arsenal had survived, Lehigh Valley wouldn't have, at least not until a new owner was found to revive the half-built and now crumbling stadium in Easton. But with the Camden Riversharks joining the league as a new franchise and Aberdeen on "hiatus," the only way for the league to maintain eight teams was to operate Lehigh Valley itself. As in 1999, the Black Diamonds would play the entire season on the road.

Wayne Krenchicki was spared that fate. Chicki became manager of the Riversharks and brought pitching coach Steve Foucault with him. Willie Upshaw moved on, too. He was hired to be the manager of the Double A Akron Aeros in the Cleveland Indians organization, but a last-minute shake-up saw him reassigned as a system-wide hitting instructor. Sparky Lyle returned to Somerset and Butch Hobson to Nashua. In Long Island, Bud Harrelson happily turned the managerial duties over to Don McCormack, and the Ducks hired Rick Wise as their new pitching coach. Tim Lindycamp left Harford Community College and took a job as a coach under manager Tommy Helms in Atlantic City.

Darrell Evans was on the shortlist to replace Willie Upshaw as manager of the Bridgeport Bluefish, but former New York Met Duffy Dyer got that job. Another possibility as a hitting instructor in the Mets organization didn't work out, and for the first time in thirty-five years, Darrell was out of the game. He tried his hand in my business, doing a little color commentary on Detroit Tigers broadcasts and worked for a start-up company in Los Angeles called the Call of Fame; former major leaguers stood by at home to take telephone calls from fans who paid by the minute on a 900 number. With Darrell out of uniform, Dan DiPace returned to retirement in Florida.

Several Arsenal alumni returned to affiliated baseball in 2001. As promised, the Texas Rangers signed David Steed to a Triple A contract in Oklahoma City. Alex Andreopoulos went to the Buffalo Bisons, the Triple A affiliate of the Cleveland Indians, and David Lundquist played with Triple A Portland (Oregon) in the San Diego Padres organization. Julien Tucker pitched 2001 in the Eastern League for Detroit's Double A team in Erie, Pennsylvania.

Johnny Isom retired from baseball. He teaches special education in Binghamton, New York, and plans to go on to graduate school. Several others also left the game, or at least disappeared off my radar screen: Victor Rosario, Jose Cepeda, Erskine Kelley, Matt Taylor, Ron Scott, Aaron Jersild, Alberto Blanco, Matt Bacon and Andy Bair.

Liam Healy went to play for the Baton Rouge Blue Marlins in the newest independent league, the All-American Association. Tyrone Horne took his ladies to the Amarillo Dillas of the independent Texas-Louisiana League. Gil Martinez did not retire; he returned to the Somerset Patriots, was traded to the Camden Riversharks and then went to play in Taiwan. Yuri Sanchez was also reported to be playing overseas.

Angel Miranda and Jose Alberro both started the year in Mexico and both returned to the Atlantic League, Miranda with Lehigh Valley and Alberro with Newark. Both of our "Italians" returned to the Atlantic League, too, under their real names this time; Chris Madonna started with the Bridgeport Bluefish and hit his way up to AA. After a brief stay in Trenton with the Red Sox AA club, Dan DiPace, Jr., played with the Nashua Pride, and then decided to return to the

Italian league. Zac Stark leaves his reading light on in the bus of the Lehigh Valley Black Diamonds. Danny Perez and Maleke Fowler patrol the outfield of the Sandcastle for the Atlantic City Surf.

Keith Lupton scoped out the possibilities of a Triple A team in York, Pennsylvania, for Maryland Baseball, and, after that fell through, went to work as a consultant for the Triple A New Orleans Zephyrs. Charlie Vascellaro landed a position with the Babe Ruth Museum in Baltimore and Adam Gladstone now works for the Tufton Group in an office in a trailer at the Ripken Stadium construction site in Aberdeen. Alison Bly, the Dyno-Mite Lady, decided that her fifth retirement tour was her last and put away the cape and the Coffin of Death.

Despite operating losses of $5,000, the Arsenal debacle did not cost Gary Helton his job. He re-upped on a one-year contract as station manager at WHFC. The station continues to grow and improve.

My spies report that the Arsenal's abrupt departure, so reminiscent of the midnight flight of the old Baltimore Colts, evaporated what little goodwill remained in the community. With luck, the ticket takers and ushers and concessionaires who worked so hard at Thomas Run Park will find better jobs at the new stadium. I should emphasize that the Ripken family is not blamed for the failure, and there is no reason to believe that the overwhelming indifference that met the Arsenal will be imposed on whatever team plays in Ripken Stadium in 2002.

While the Aberdeen Arsenal enjoyed the life span of a June bug, the Atlantic League in particular and independent baseball in general are thriving. Enthusiasm spawned a brand-new league in 2001, the All-American Association, though early returns suggest severe growing pains. Much more promising news came from Newark, where the Bears made national headlines by signing longtime big-leaguers Jim Leyritz, Lance Johnson, Jaime Navarro and Jack Armstrong plus both Jose and Ozzie Canseco. "I had no clue what the Atlantic League was until I saw Jose on TV," said Leyritz. "I was going crazy at home, and my wife was ready to throw me out of the house. I knew I wasn't ready to give it up yet." Leyritz signed a Triple A contract just a couple of weeks later, Jose Canseco hooked on as a DH for the Chicago White Sox and former Atlantic City Surf Ruben Sierra revived his major league career with the Texas Rangers. The Chicago Cubs considered Bobby Hill's year in the Atlantic League developmental enough to start him out in Double A, on the fast track to the big time. Though it was unable to avoid the financial problems that have afflicted other independent leagues, it looks as if the Atlantic League will continue to provide hundreds of ballplayers the opportunity to make a living with gloves and bats for a little longer yet. A very few will prove themselves and fight their way to the majors; many more will, I hope, be able to leave the game and get on with their lives, knowing that they gave it every chance.

A couple of weeks after the season ended, I returned to NPR News in time to anchor the last two presidential debates. Afterward, the stamina I developed in baseball proved extremely helpful when I was called upon to provide play by play of electoral extra innings and the deliberations of the Florida and United States Supreme Courts. I have been able to retain that nice warm note, too, and it turns out that I'm able to recap the news as well as the scoring.

But I learned a great deal more than a few technical skills. The guys taught me to have faith in young people; the kids are all right. Baseball taught me patience: it's a long season. It also taught me not to waste my time anymore; I vow to dither no longer. It was immensely satisfying to take on such a steep learning curve and succeed. I will always remember the roof of the press box at Thomas Run Park with happiness and pride. I will always have another life in baseball, too, even if I never get another chance to do it every day. I will treasure another set of friends. And the demise of the team, sad as it was, means I will always be the one and only Voice of the Aberdeen Arsenal.

The experience taught me to take risks again. The more I think about it, the more I believe that baseball was my last chance. If I hadn't done it, I fear I might have drowned. Somewhere along the way, I found my passion again. Passion for baseball, it turned out, translated into passion for radio, and renewed interest in life in general.

Several months after the season ended, I ran into a guy in Baltimore who said he'd been a regular listener to Arsenal games. When I expressed polite skepticism, he cited a couple of my lines to prove it. When I then asked if he was just a base-ball fanatic or whether he had a relative on the team, he said, neither: "I enjoyed listening because it was so obvious that you were having a great time." He was dead right. I loved it. I loved the team, I loved the roof, I loved the game, I loved my headset, I loved being on the radio three or four hours every day. Early in the season, I prayed for rainouts, just to get a lit-tle rest, but by the end, I hated the off days and wondered what I would do with myself after the season was over.

When I got back to doing news, the thrill was still there. Obviously, I didn't have a team to root for, but I cared a lot more than I had just six months earlier. I was nervous and confident at the same time, excited about being on the air again and eager to use my wonderful new tools. Getting out of the cocoon revived my spirit and, not so coincidentally, my career. After play by play, I knew I needed to find a way to be on the radio every day. At this writing, it looks as if I will be offered the opportunity to host a daily two-hour national call-in show, which would be a great chance to use my skills back in the big leagues. I will, however, insist on a baseball clause in my contract: if Mr. Steinbrenner calls, I'm gone.

Acknowledgments

*I*n the days when I covered police stories in New York, cops of many ethnicities described a senior officer who provided advice and professional contacts as their "rabbi." Ron Shapiro is my rabbi in the baseball business. For reasons he alone can explain, this superagent, a man who arranges multimillion-dollar deals for ballplayers and somewhat less lucrative contracts for broadcasters, went out of his way to arrange a volunteer job for a stranger. He provided opportunity, encouragement and criticism, and when the time came, he was instrumental in the development of this book. I am eternally grateful for his help and his friendship.

I also owe a great debt to my friends and colleagues at National Public Radio. Cadi Simon was the first person to suggest that I write about my experiences in the Arsenal radio booth. She proposed a series of biweekly commentaries, which we titled "Play by Play" and, as my editor, helped me find the right tone and subject material. Ellen McDonnell, executive producer of *Morning Edition*, agreed to put my stories on the air and after detecting a ponderous note in my delivery, provided a well-timed piece of advice: "Hey, this ain't Bosnia.

Lighten up." After Cadi was diverted by other responsibilities, Jeffrey Katz picked up the editorial baton. Several of the stories in this book germinated on *Morning Edition*.

My bosses, Bruce Drake and Barbara Rehm, had every right to be exasperated by my unreasonable and sudden request for a long leave of absence, but were instead helpful and supportive. Bud Aiello and Bill Hineman of NPR's technical staff provided invaluable advice and assistance.

Three days before I left for Aberdeen and baseball, I told Noah Adams why I'd be away that summer and he was the first to suggest that there might be a book in it. He contacted his editor, Steve Ross, who had just taken the helm at Crown Books and despite, or perhaps because of, the fact that Steve quit smoking that day, he liked the idea. Working first with Ron Shapiro and then later with David Black, the marvelous agent to whom Ron referred me (another favor I owe him), Steve completed the deal quickly and painlessly. It would never have been a book, however, without the efforts of my editor at Crown, Doug Pepper, who understood what I was doing better than I did and helped me transform an inchoate jumble of anecdotes and interviews into a narrative.

Late in the season, a photographer named David Deal showed up at an Arsenal home game. After visiting minor league parks around the country for the past three years, he said he was just about ready to put together a book of art photography. He'd heard some of my pieces on *Morning Edition* and asked if I'd consider writing an introduction to his book. Naturally, I put this off until a deadline loomed, but seeing his superb photographs at a presentation at a Washington bookstore was a reinspiration. The process of writing this book began with the process of writing that introduction. It was a great privilege to be included in *Prospects:* those interested can see examples of David Deal's work on his Web site at www.DavidDeal.com.

I have to thank Peter Kirk of Maryland Baseball and Jon Danos, general manager of the Bowie Baysox, who gave me my first chance. Dave Collins, the Voice of the Baysox, taught me his craft and much else, besides, and the listeners of WNAV-AM, Annapolis, put up with my many mistakes. Maryland Baseball's Keith Lupton, the general manager of the Arsenal, was bold enough to hire a rank outsider to broadcast his team's games.

Gary Helton, the manager of WHFC-FM, Bel Air, made the risky decision to put me and the Arsenal on the radio and I am especially grateful to him and all the other board operators who made our electronic shoestring work so well.

Charlie Vascellaro, the Arsenal's publicity director, provided solutions to most of my problems; the tough ones he handed off to his able interns Karaline Jackson and Spencer Castillo. Charlie's meticulously maintained records proved critical when I needed to reconstruct statistics and standings. I would also like to thank James Keller of Howe Sportsdata for kind permission to use the standings at the head of each chapter and Jeffrey Wilson of *Baseball America*, who helped me track down information about the game in Taiwan.

I owe a great deal to my play by play colleagues and to the journalists who covered the Atlantic League. Over the season, I shamelessly stole their material for use on the air at every opportunity. In this book, their material is cited in the text, except for two quotes about the Nashua Pride lifted from articles written by Tom King in the *Nashua Telegraph* and a couple more about the Lehigh Valley Black Diamonds taken from a column by Paul Sokoloski of the *Express-Times*. I am also in debt to Tom Eberwein of the *Aegis* for his excellent coverage of the Arsenal during and especially after the season.

My host family, Ed and Georgette Paulson, opened their home, their hearts and their refrigerator. Their grandchildren, Becca and Seth, reminded me daily of life beyond baseball, and taught me how to play Bugdom, the game that came with my computer. Ron Scott, my housemate in Aberdeen, helped me schlep the radio equipment to and from the bus at both ends of every road trip. Arsenal clubhouse manager Donald Lebrun did some of that heavy lifting, too.

Writing a book proved to be very, very different from writing even long radio pieces. I leaned heavily on two readers for encouragement, feedback and reality checks: my wife, Liane, and my old friend Sam Chapin. Both know me well enough to tell me when I'm making an idiot of myself and did so, frequently. In the end, Sam also provided a refuge at his summer home in Plymouth, Massachusetts, where I struggled through a rewrite in idyllic surroundings. Research librarian Kee Malesky did a non-baseball fact check for me. All of the above caught errors of fact, judgment and style; any that remain are my responsibility alone.

Most of all, I want to thank the players, coaches and staff of the Aberdeen Arsenal and the Atlantic League for sharing their season, their stories and their companionship.

About the Author

For twenty-five years, NEAL CONAN served as a utility infielder at National Public Radio, juggling the duties of reporter, editor and producer in New York, Washington and London. His assignments took him to most of the countries of Europe, much of the Middle East and to many parts of the United States. More recently, he won a spot in NPR's regular lineup as host of *Talk of the Nation*, which he started on September 10, 2001. He and his wife, Liane Hansen, live in Bethesda, Maryland. They have two children.